Making Friends With Your Unconscious Mind: The User Friendly Guide

Patricia O'Hanlon Hudson, Ph.D.

Co-Author of
Rewriting Love Stories

The Center Press   Omaha, Nebraska

Library of Congress Cataloging-in-Publication Data

Hudson, Patricia O'Hanlon, Ph.D.

Making friends with your unconscious mind: the user friendly guide / Patricia O'Hanlon Hudson, Ph.D.

"The Center Press"
Includes bibliographical references and index.
ISBN 0-963-4886-1-9

The Center Press • 11926 Arbor Street • Omaha, NE 68144

Acknowledgments

So many people have given me helpful feedback over the years of working on this book that I hardly know where to begin. I fear I will leave someone out, but here goes.

Many thanks to: John Simpson, Paul Lambakis, Steve Gilligan, Denise Ross, Bob and Mary Britchford, Suzy and Paul Landow, Loretta Calabro, Lorraine Cornish, Liz Kofoed, Tom Pansing, Carolyn Shulo, Linda Schaefer, Frank Butler, and Terry Moore who all read the book and made corrections.

Sandy Kutler, Julie Jurich, Mary Neumann and Ed Cummings made extra efforts in helping me to publish and were supportive over the extended time it took to bring this to the presses.

There are others to whom gratitude is owed, including my graduate adviser, George Marx, but I have tried to at least remember the top dozen or so. Thank you to all the staff at the Hudson Center who supported and encouraged me and put up with the time it took to get this book ready to publish.

Thank you to Judith Serevino and Robert Cain who edited the book for me and to Bridget Weide whose computer skills were crucial for this production.

Thanks also to my older sons, Nick and Zack Hexum, to my daughter, Angie Hexum, and her soon-to-be-husband, David Pope, who were helpful in editing, and to my youngest son, Patrick, who tolerated my presence at the keyboard well.

I am eternally grateful to my father, Lofton Hudson, for backing me all the way on this project and throughout my life, and to Rhonda Applegarth, my business manager, who really is my life manager, without whom this book would have been hidden in my computer for years.

Words are not adequate to express the gratitude I feel to have the support of my delightful, witty, loving partner and husband, Bill O'Hanlon. It is possible that the dream of writing this book might have come true without him but having him in my life makes this and many other dreams come true.

—Pat Hudson

CONTENTS

CHAPTER 1

WHAT IS THE PROGRAM?

THE USES OF THE UNCONSCIOUS MIND

I became interested in the unconscious mind when I entered college in 1963. As a child, learning to read was difficult for me. The principal of my high school had told me that I was not college material, so I was afraid of failure as I went to college. I decided to go to a friend of my father's in Kansas City, a physician hypnotherapist named James Rowland, to see if he could help me become a better student. My high school record was mediocre. I had never received even a single "A" for a semester grade.

With Dr. Rowland's help, I developed skills in self-hypnosis and was transformed from a frustrated high school student into a college student who graduated with honors. These skills helped me in my master's and doctoral programs where, with the exception of statistics, I maintained straight "A's." My experience demonstrates just how radically people can change their self-images and skills as students. Now I take particular pleasure as a psychologist in working with frustrated struggling students and non-students struggling with the frustrations of everyday life. I enjoy helping them to discover and use the inner skills they did not know they had.

Since my first experience with self-hypnosis in the 1960s, I have been a student of the unconscious mind. During these years, I have discovered invaluable inner resources for changing myself and helping my clients change. Using the methods of hypnosis, self-hypnosis, and dream analysis, I was able to become friends with my unconscious. In my practice, I share these skills with others in order that they can experience the freedom and power to accomplish what they want with the help of their unconscious minds. These skills seemed easy for others to learn in classes I have held for the public, so I decided to make them available in book form.

In teaching classes in self-hypnosis and dream analysis, I found that some of my students were afraid of the unconscious mind. Because I spent so many years treating the unconscious as a friend and helpmate, I am always surprised to realize that many people see the unconscious as something to be feared. They have the late-show-on-television attitude that evil deeds and sinister thoughts lurk beneath the level of consciousness. As you read this book and practice these techniques, you are going to find that nothing could be farther from the truth.

The apprehensions people have about their unconscious minds are similar to the apprehensions many have about computers. When beginners sit down at the computer, they are fearful that they will do something wrong and ruin everything. A similar fear of making some big mistake arises for many people when first getting to know their unconscious minds.

My first two goals for you, as you become friends with your unconscious mind, are to eliminate this fear of the unknown and to encourage you to integrate the use of your unconscious mind in order for it to become as much a part of you as using your hands to eat. Treating part of your mental processes as alien to you is as illogical as treating some part of your body as alien and unacceptable.

Becoming familiar with a computer can help you retrieve information and accomplish things quickly and easily. The unconscious can do exactly the same thing for you. Your unconscious can help you retrieve, input or delete information.

How do you know if you need to have the help of your unconscious? In the Bible, Paul says, "I do not understand what I do; for I don't do what I would like to do, but instead I do what I hate." (Romans 7:15) That is what we all experience when we have not received the cooperation of our unconscious minds. Often, in spite of our conscious desire to change some unproductive or harmful behavior, we find ourselves repeatedly doing what seems to be destructive.

That demonstrates our need to have help from our unconscious minds.

I have been discussing the need to get in touch with your unconscious, but you may not realize that it is often trying to get in touch with you. For example, when you have vivid dreams, particularly when they are repetitive or frightening, your unconscious may be trying to get a message through to your conscious mind. If you keep dreaming that your spouse is ailing when he or she is healthy, that might be a warning from your unconscious that the relationship is ailing and needs attention.

When you find yourself repeatedly acting in a counter-productive way, that too may be an attempt by the unconscious to reach you. If you have found yourself choosing again and again to develop relationships with abusive people, that might be a signal from your unconscious that you need to deal with some particular issue, such as your relationship with one of your parents. Just as a file on a computer disk may need to be erased, ideas that were programmed by childhood experiences may need to be deleted from your unconscious.

Recently, I had a young woman client who had been raped. She came to me because she chose men who mistreated her. Under hypnosis, the woman discovered that she continued the cycle of selecting negative men because the rape made her feel like damaged goods, unworthy of a kind man. While this sort of work is easier if you seek a therapist, it is not impossible to do by yourself.

Have you ever made a decision that others labeled irrational only to later realize that the decision seemed to come from an inner wisdom? During my first year of college, under the strong influence of a friend of my parents, I joined a sorority. I became president of the pledge class. Every Wednesday night, the night of the pledge meeting, I began having headaches. Finally, I realized that the headaches came from the unconscious knowledge that this was the wrong decision for me. When I announced my decision to leave the sorority, the Dean of Women and many other people put pressure on me to remain in the sorority. This pressure reached absurd levels when the Dean of Women told me that people left sororities only because of sexual misconduct; if I left my sorority, my morals would be under suspicion. They apparently were convinced that my decision was a mistake. I stuck to my decision, and I have never regretted it. After acknowledging what was bothering me and taking action, the headaches stopped. Had I already mastered self-hypnosis and dream analysis, this issue might have been resolved much sooner or perhaps in a different way. Dreams, repetitive unwanted behaviors, and physical symptoms, such as headaches and stomachaches, often are examples of the unconscious reaching out to our conscious minds. A friend of mine joked, "Everything from asthma to zits can be a message from your unconscious!"

Mastering self-hypnosis and dream analysis can simply make life easier. Perhaps I would have been able to become a good student in college by consciously making a great deal of effort, but learning to concentrate and improve my memory and test-taking skills through self-hypnosis certainly made the process much easier. The help of the unconscious by interpretation of dreams and the practice of self-hypnosis can create a simple, more effortless life. This can be accomplished through relaxation, improvement in self-esteem, eliminating phobias, releasing creativity, and decreasing pain.

Relaxation through self-hypnosis is a powerful tool and is one of the main reasons people want to learn this skill. By mastering relaxation, you can improve your general health by decreasing your reactions to stress. Hypnosis and self-hypnosis have helped patients with a wide variety of specific symptoms, from warts to asthma. Often the relaxing imagery alone can encourage the healing process by removing the interfering physiology of tension. My general strategy in working with patients with physical problems is to use hypnosis to get initial improvement and then support that improvement by teaching the clients to use self-hypnosis and, in some situations, dream analysis. You do not need a therapist, however, to get started using these techniques.

The use of self-hypnosis for pain control can be dramatic. Often we reach the limits of what medications can do for the pain we experience or we wish to avoid drugs because of their side effects. This is the point at which self-hypnosis can help us decrease the pain which we experience and change our relationship to it. Through dreams you can discover if the symptom is serving a purpose and ask for a change in the symptom. I have successfully treated various physical difficulties such as a slipped disk, blurred vision, high blood pressure, chronic inoperable pain, and post-operative pain. I never advocate hypnosis and self-hypnosis as a substitute for medical treatment; however, hypnosis and self-hypnosis can be helpful in relieving symptoms or in promoting healing through relaxation and relief of stress.

Another way the unconscious mind helps us is by facilitating our creativity. We may spontaneously get ideas upon awakening or have dreams that give us creative ideas. When people say, "I'll sleep on it," frequently they are turning the problem over to their unconscious minds to generate a creative solution. The night before I plan to write or outline a speech, I will review the general topic to be covered and then ask my unconscious to organize the material in a useful way while I sleep. When I wake up, it seems as if the material has fallen into place during the night.

Interesting accounts of scientific breakthroughs demonstrate the input of the unconscious. Auguste Kekule, a chemist, had a dream of snakes swirling around in front of him while he was sitting in front of a fire. The snakes began to bite their own tails. That image gave Kekule the insight that the chemical structure of benzene was closed rather than open. Kekule won the Nobel Prize for the discovery of the benzene ring.

**SIGNS THAT YOU NEED
HELP FROM YOUR
UNCONSCIOUS**

Difficulty concentrating

Performance problems

Habits that need changing

Reactions to stress

Repetitive dreams

Physical symptoms

Need for creativity

In the area of artistic creativity, I have had painters and composers tell me that they get ideas for their creations from their sleep. Clearly, the unconscious has a variety of uses that have always been available to you. If you have felt better after a dream, if you have been able to concentrate deeply on something, if you have rested for a few minutes and gotten over a headache, if you have been talking to a friend and been amazed at how quickly the time passed, or if you have been reading a novel oblivious to what was going on around you, then you have already been using the resources of your unconscious. The purpose of this book is to help you have these natural skills readily available to you. If you are ready to reduce your stress, handle fears, get over the past, understand yourself, change your habits, and maybe even your life, then read on!

SUMMARY: The unconscious can be a great help to you. Signs that you need this help include repeating unwanted behaviors, stress symptoms, physical symptoms, feeling blocked creatively, and repetitive unpleasant dreams. The techniques in this book will help you become friends with your unconscious to get its support in making changes or in resolving painful issues.

EXERCISE: Buy a loose-leaf notebook to keep track of the changes in your relationship with your unconscious as you master these techniques. Divide the notebook into four sections: General Journal, Self-hypnosis, Dreams, and Discussion. Under "General" make a list of the times you now realize that your unconscious was trying to send you a message through symptoms or feelings. Write on another piece of paper repetitive dreams or themes of dreams from the past and file that under "Dreams" for your future exploration.

CHAPTER 2

THE UNCONSCIOUS IS AS NEUTRAL AS A COMPUTER

DEVELOPING A DEFINITION OF THE UNCONSCIOUS MIND

The term "unconscious" was used in the 1880s, even before the time of Freud's interest in the unconscious. Pierre Janet, a French psychiatrist, was the first to use the term "subconscious." (I prefer the term "unconscious" to the term "subconscious" because the prefix "sub" implies "less" or "under" thinking. Perhaps thanks to the "uncola," "un" has a less negative connotation.) Freud and Janet had opposing points of view in their time. Janet thought that psychologically healthy people did not have unconscious minds, while Freud demonstrated the normal activity of the unconscious through everyday experiences such as slips of the tongue, dreams, humor, and creativity. Freud saw the unconscious as the storehouse for unacceptable impulses and thoughts. These days, the unconscious is more commonly seen as a positive resource. The creative hypnotherapist, Milton H. Erickson, M.D., had much to do with making this shift. He believed the unconscious generated solutions from its storehouse of abilities and creativity.

In my own work with clients, I don't usually start with direct intervention in the unconscious using hypnosis and dreamwork. I generally begin with having the client *do something different*. This conscious intervention of changing behavior is often enough to bring about change. However, when this straightforward approach does not work, I use techniques to get help from the unconscious, usually hypnosis and, less often, dreamwork. With some clients, I teach self-hypnosis and assign daily practice of a certain amount of time each day, such as fifteen minutes. I use this technique for clients who want to change in a variety of ways: to modify habits, such as smoking or eating behaviors; to change their performance of some activity such as studying or public speaking; or to control a physical symptom.

What defines the term "unconscious"? A relationship exists between the unconscious mind and conscious memories. Some psychologists who study the process of memory have found that we have two types of memory: short-term and long-term. Short-term memories are those memories of the recent past which are effortlessly available to us. They can be a new experience, such as a piece of information that we just learned, or it can be information pulled out of the long-term memory. For example, if I asked you to tell me the make of your first automobile, even though it was probably not in your mind as you were reading, it may have now transferred from your long-term memory (unconscious) to your short-term memory (consciousness). The term "unconscious" can refer to the long-term storage bank from which information can be retrieved.

The various meanings of the term "unconscious" tend to fall into two categories. The first category refers to mental processes that are below awareness, and the second category generally refers to the unconscious as a storehouse. In this book, the term unconscious will refer to a storehouse of resources, memories, and abilities. These abilities may create change or prevent change. Because we cannot always consciously open this storage area, we have to use techniques such as self-hypnosis, imagery, and interpretation of dreams to open those doors.

THE QUALITIES OF THE UNCONSCIOUS

Books on dreams usually take the stance that dreams never lie. I feel that you cannot always count on the unconscious for accurate information, not because of its attempt to deceive, but because of certain qualities of the unconscious.

The first quality is that the unconscious is not rational. Due sometimes to early programming, the unconscious will hold a belief that, as perceived by your conscious mind, does not make sense. For example, competent adults can feel plagued with doubts and feel like an impostor because of unconscious beliefs instilled during their childhoods.

In hypnosis, there is a phenomenon called trance logic. This is the ability of the unconscious to hold completely contradictory points of view. For example, the unconscious might hold the same information as being true and not true, or the opposing attitudes that the individual unconsciously wants to die and wants not to die, simultaneously.

There can be two-way communication between the outside world and the unconscious and between the body and the unconscious. The information flowing in either direction can be liberating or limiting, valuing or devaluing.

Sometimes communications that flow into the unconscious relate to how we will be in the future. When I went through hypnotherapy many years ago to become a better student, I learned that one of the reasons I had not been a good student was that, as a young child, I had overheard my mother say that she was concerned that I would never learn to read. As a result, I took that as programming that I **could not** read. It is as though we are often in a trance in our daily life and suggestions can enter our unconscious minds causing us to make predictions about our future.

This two-way communication with the unconscious explains why you can develop either positive or negative self-images by information coming from your unconscious or into your unconscious. In my own life, an example of a message that came into and now out of my unconscious is, "Can't is not in your vocabulary." This was something my father repeatedly said to me. This suggestion was probably an excellent way to create an over-achiever. It just took awhile to sink in. I do feel that almost anything I want to accomplish is possible, partially because of this input into and, in recent history, from my unconscious.

Two other qualities of the unconscious, as these examples demonstrate, are its ability to receive information, at some times more readily than others, and the enhanced ability to receive information through repetition. In the case of overhearing my mother's prediction, as a seven-year-old I had been in a receptive mode because I had come downstairs from my bedroom after being put to bed for the night when I overheard her comment. This drowsy state may have made me more receptive. In the case of the "can't"-is-not-in-your-vocabulary message, repetition was the key to entering my unconscious.

The ability to program yourself by repetition can be useful. We can deliberately put messages into the unconscious by affirmations. Repeating positive phrases, such as "I am a competent and caring person," puts positive information into the unconscious.

Two-way communication with the unconscious can be seen in response to involuntary bodily functions. In other words, some things happen without our consciously choosing them to happen. Mind-body communications can **come from** the inside, as in physical symptoms to express guilt, anger, or grief, or the information can **go into** the unconscious, as in healing through imagery.

Another involuntary experience that comes from the unconscious is dreaming. We know through research that dreaming spontaneously occurs four or five times a night. As I have already mentioned, that can be a message from the unconscious trying to get you to pay attention to something or it can simply be the way your unconscious has of dealing with whatever is occurring in your waking life.

Ideomotor behaviors, such as the hand rising automatically at the hypnotherapist's suggestion, are involuntary physical movements that occur in trance. These offer further evidence of information coming from the unconscious. In hypnosis, the hypnotherapist can ask for certain movements to occur, such as a hand levitation or a finger being raised, as a signal for an answer from the unconscious. Subjects reported that the hand raising seemed to be spontaneous and that they felt that they were not consciously making it happen. You need not be concerned about ideomotor behaviors with self-hypnosis.

Although the unconscious is primarily helpful and a great resource for change, it does have elements that can contribute to occasionally sending confusing information to our conscious minds. I notice that there are times when we are working with computers that this neutral machine seems "out to get us." When we work with the unconscious we could get that feeling about the unconscious too. The best way to clarify when inaccurate or unhelpful communication is coming from or getting into the unconscious is to talk to your unconscious. You can't influence your unconscious without communication just as you cannot influence your computer without being able to communicate with it. Friendship provides the best vehicle for that influence.

MAKING FRIENDS WITH YOUR UNCONSCIOUS

A fellow therapist, Mark Lehrer, suggests that when you make a friend of your unconscious mind, you use the same strategies that you would use when making friends with people. If you were in a new work environment and wanted to establish relationships with your co-workers, you might find yourself trying to be open-minded and patient with them, not critical and competitive. You might listen carefully to them. If they did not do what you wanted them to, you would probably not yell at them, but you might ask yourself how you could encourage them. The same methods that work well with people will help you establish a friendly relationship with your unconscious. You may have noticed that certain settings work best for establishing friendships. Often these are quiet places that allow interaction. In becoming friends with your unconscious, you also will want to choose a place that is quiet and relatively free from distractions. Once you have a working relationship with your unconscious, the setting becomes less and less important. After years of experience, I can go into a good trance sitting in an airport terminal or on an airplane, have a dream, and interpret it before I land.

In order to get to know people, you have to spend time with them. This is true of the unconscious as well. You do have to be willing to take the time to practice the skills you will need in order to master these techniques. You may know the ancient joke about the young man hurrying down a New York street with a violin under his arm. He asks an old man, "How do I get to Carnegie Hall?" The old man answers, "Practice, practice, practice!" The more you develop these resources and experiment with the technique that works best for you, the more skilled you will become. You may have noticed that in situations where you spend a lot of time with people, such as at work, you begin to be friends with them even though they might not have initially seemed to have had much in common with you. Familiarity seems to breed comfort, not contempt.

The time of day you practice will depend upon which technique you are perfecting. With self-hypnosis and meditation, you may want to designate some time when you are not likely to fall asleep. With dream programming, you will need some time just before you go to sleep to write down a few thoughts about your dream goal. Writing down your dreams takes a few minutes when you first awaken. (There is a method you can use for this provided in Chapter 5.) With interpretation of dreams, you may want to have a time with a partner who shares your interest in interpretation.

Now that you have an idea of what time, place, and attitude will serve you best, you have my best wishes for success as you venture into your unconscious mind.

SUMMARY: The term "unconscious" can mean different things, ranging from "unaware" to "unable to respond." In this book, the "unconscious" refers to the storage place for abilities, memories, and solutions to many of life's dilemmas.

The unconscious has a two-way communication quality for information to get into and out of the unconscious. The unconscious is not necessarily logical and can hold totally contradictory beliefs. The best way to manage these unusual qualities of the unconscious is to become friends with the unconscious. Strategies for becoming friends with the unconscious are the same as the strategies you would use to become friends with another person.

EXERCISE: In your journal, under the "Discussion" section, write down any strong inconsistencies, like consciously wanting to do something, but botching it, that you think might be an example of your unconscious holding illogical and contradictory views.

Deliberately add information to your unconscious by writing down a daily affirmation, something positive to say to yourself. Repeat this phrase every time you eat or drink and as you go to sleep at night.

CHAPTER 3

BOOTING UP THE PROGRAM

Turning on your home computer is useless unless you can get it to start doing something. This is called "booting up" the program. Getting access to the hypnosis program of your unconscious mind is very much like learning to boot up a program on a computer. When someone first hears the words "boot up the program," they often become apprehensive and concerned that somehow they are going to mess up this very expensive tool. I certainly had this fear when I first sat down at a computer. I will, hopefully, dispel similar fears and clear up misconceptions that are popularly held about hypnosis. I will discuss the characteristics of a good hypnotic subject, the hypnotic experience, and the way to put yourself into a trance.

FEARS AND MYTHS ABOUT HYPNOSIS

In many ways, doing self-hypnosis instead of being hypnotized by others will eliminate some of the typical fears. For example, many people fear that if they are hypnotized, they will be under someone's power and, therefore, could do something immoral. The idea that you would do something in a trance that you would not normally do, or that is against your morality, is incorrect. This idea, promoted in movies and on television, makes for interesting fictional plots but has little to do with reality.

Another common misconception is that you lose self-control under hypnosis. This notion comes from "stage hypnosis" featured in nightclubs. While the person being hypnotized does become more open to suggestion and pays less attention to considerations of reality, he does not lose self-control. The use of self-hypnosis should dispel this fear because you are the one in charge. Are you likely to tell yourself to do something you would feel stupid about later? No. When subjects, often after drinking a few alcoholic beverages, volunteer to go up on stage and be hypnotized, that is a very different context than when students of self-hypnosis deliberately sit down and ask their unconscious minds for assistance. As one of my students pointed out, many people who quack like a duck "under trance" on stage would be willing to quack on other occasions as well.

Another fear that some people have is that they will not come out of trance. I have hypnotized over a thousand people and have yet to have someone not come out of trance. Some other veteran hypnotherapists have reported to me that some of their clients have experienced a delay in coming out of trance. The worst case scenario is that the person "sleeps it off" after a few hours. In my twenty-five years of doing self-hypnosis, I have occasionally fallen asleep during trance and have had a refreshing nap. I assume that the unconscious continues to do its work while my conscious mind rests, and, so far, I have no evidence to the contrary.

How does self-hypnosis differ from sleep? Will you be unaware of what is going on around you? Self-hypnosis is a form of heightened concentration, not an absence of awareness. The brain wave patterns of sleep are very different from the brain wave patterns of hypnosis. The patterns of hypnosis are mostly like a pattern of concentration. Although you often feel as though you have had a pleasant nap when you use self-hypnosis, you do not usually go to sleep and you are likely to be aware of noises around you.

Another fear that people have is that they will not remember what has occurred in trance. While it does sometimes happen that my clients have amnesia concerning what occurred under trance, it is likely and, indeed, more common that they will remember all that occurred. Since in self-hypnosis you are unquestionably in control of the process, you are likely to create the kind of experience that you want. When you are your own guide, you have control over the destination.

People often think that being able to be hypnotized means that they are weak-willed. The respected Stanford University psychologist, Ernest Hilgard, has studied the characteristics of good hypnotic subjects and found evidence contrary to this "weak-willed" idea. The characteristics of a person who goes more easily into trance are high motivation, optimism, enthusiasm, receptivity to the ideas of others, and the ability to visualize. Good subjects tend to have concentration skills and average or above average intelligence.

Sometimes, when I mention that visualization is helpful, people report that they are not good at creating mental images. I have found two exercises helpful in improving visualization. The first is to look at a picture and then to close your eyes and practice re-creating that picture in your mind. Check the picture again and repeat the creation in your mind. The second exercise is to sit in front of the television set with your eyes closed and practice making up the images on the screen from the sounds you hear. Like any skill, visualization improves with practice.

I suggest that you not be concerned with exactly how good a subject you are. Going into trance deeply is not necessary to gain the benefits that you might want in self-hypnosis, so please do not get stuck wondering if you are or are not a good subject. It is like wondering if you are or are not a good traveler before you go on your first journey. Go on the trip and discover what is possible.

WHAT DOES IT FEEL LIKE TO BE IN TRANCE?

Keep in mind that we all have experienced trance in our daily lives. If you have been watching television and did not hear someone call your name, that was an everyday trance. When you were absorbed in a lecture, a church service, or a conversation and were unaware of the time, that was natural trance. The unpleasant experience of being called upon in school and having no idea what the teacher was even discussing was also trance.

In my classes on self-hypnosis, after everyone has the experience of being hypnotized, they report a wide variety of responses. Many say that their hands felt different—tingly, heavy, or light. Most report that they felt much as they do when they are daydreaming, which is an example of natural trance. Some report that trance is similar to the concentration of prayer. Almost all the people in the class report that they found the experience to be relaxing. Each of us may experience being in trance in our own unique way. You will probably feel relaxed and you may have some different bodily sensations. Also, you are likely to concentrate sharply on the thoughts, images, and memories inside your mind. For most people, trances are a familiar state, and they do not separate them from the external world.

I want to encourage you to approach trances with an open mind and not force any certain experience. Being open to experimentation and discovery is the best way to find what is possible for you.

WHAT IS HYPNOSIS?

Since hypnosis does not have a clearly measurable difference from concentration in terms of brain wave patterns, defining hypnosis has been difficult. Hilgard, in an attempt to define the state of hypnosis, suggests the following characteristics.

First, subjects sit still, letting the hypnotist tell them what to do, such as taking deep breaths. Generally, the subjects experience relaxed feelings.

Second, subjects focus their attention upon what the hypnotist suggests. Typically, the hypnotist will suggest that subjects notice their own sensations such as their breathing, specific sounds in the room, or the feelings of the chairs under their bodies.

The third characteristic of hypnosis is a marked enhancement of recalling memories, creating images, or creating entire fantasies. For example, in trance you might ask yourself to recall the first time you did some activity, such as ride a bicycle, and have that memory return to your conscious mind. With the imagery of hypnosis, some challenging activity, such as asking for a raise, giving a speech, or controlling a habit, would be easier. I have had marked success in working with several athletes who wanted to improve their performances. Imagination seems to be a very powerful facilitator of action. Maxwell Maltz, the author of *Psychocybernetics*, says that if we cannot imagine doing something, then we cannot do it. Imagining succeeding in any task is the first step to accomplishing it.

A fourth characteristic of hypnosis is that the subjects stop paying much attention to considerations of reality. For example, when using hypnosis for pain control, suggesting that some part of the body has the experience of being numb as with Novocain might seem silly or impossible to people out of trance, but this is a technique commonly used very successfully in hypnosis.

Hilgard noted that a fifth characteristic of hypnosis is that subjects become more open to suggestion and will adopt and enact roles suggested by the hypnotherapist. For example, if a subject lacked confidence in some task, the hypnotherapist might suggest that the subject think of someone who is good at that task. Then the subject would imagine exactly how the expert would act. The person in trance would then imagine doing exactly the same task in the same way. Then the hypnotherapist would suggest that the subject would find it much easier and more comfortable to do the task the next time the opportunity arose. Finally, a person in trance may not recall what happened during hypnosis, particularly if there is a suggestion for amnesia (forgetting). As I mentioned before, this is unlikely in self-hypnosis.

My clients usually report that they experience trance as very relaxing and comfortable. This, too, is my experience with self-hypnosis. Most of my clients have a sense that they could get up and walk out of the room if they wanted to. (However, no one has yet. Thank goodness!) Occasionally, clients will not remember what happened during trance. Trance tends to be such an enjoyable experience that being upset by not recalling exactly what occurred does not usually happen.

Often I will hear, as do my clients, outside noises while I am in trance. I suggest to myself and to them that noticing these sounds will only deepen the trance. Using this suggestion helps the noises contribute to, not distract from, the trance. At times a very loud noise had occurred in the office building during a hypnosis session. When I later apologized to the client for it, the client reported never having heard it. Sometimes people hear outside noises, but typically they ignore them to the point of not hearing them.

Many people in trance notice interesting sensations in their hands, as I mentioned earlier. Some report that their hands feel either light, heavy, or tingly. Some report that they felt as if their hands were missing. Personally, as I go deeper into trance, I have less and less awareness of my body. Sometimes, during self-hypnosis, I have almost experienced a sensation of "pure spirit," a total lack of body. Self-hypnosis is like the experience of lying in bed awake, but very physically relaxed, while the mind is active. I have often found dozing in the back of a car on a long trip to be a very trance-inducing experience, that is, having a relaxed body and focused mind.

My clients have also reported to me that they see colors while they are in trance and that the colors change with the depth and length of the trance. The experience of trance is an individualized experience. You cannot "do it wrong." While you should be aware of what you might reasonably expect, I hesitate to describe trance in too much detail because I want you to simply enjoy whatever you experience.

WHAT IS HYPNOSIS?

Relaxation

Focused attention

Enhanced ability to recall

Use of the imagination

Increased suggestibility

Brain wave pattern of concentration

GENERAL PRINCIPLES OF GOING INTO TRANCE

I am the director of a counseling center where most of the staff members are trained in hypnosis. One of our staff members, in preparing for a speech on self-hypnosis to a local organization, asked each of us how we do self-hypnosis. One invariable principle for us all was to begin by changing our breathing. All of us used slow, deep breaths to start trances for ourselves.

Generally, relaxing and letting go helps create a trance. If you have never consciously tried to relax, tense up your body as tightly as you can and then try to get all your muscles to relax at once. Tensing and relaxing sections of your body progressively, for example, one leg and then the other, etc., helps you to experience the difference between tension and relaxation.

Using your imagination helps you to go into trance and may help deepen the experience. To deepen the experience, imagine a relaxing place, a time during which you relaxed earlier in your life, going down stairs, or going down in an elevator. (I will specifically outline these methods in more detail later in this chapter.)

In many ways, going into trance is like getting your conscious mind out of the way. I suggest, therefore, that you do not try too hard to make anything happen, but just allow whatever happens to happen. The expression "go with the flow" describes this state of mind.

There is no right or wrong way to go into trance, so just keep experimenting. I had one client who found that she could go into a deep trance only while taking a warm bath. On very rare occasions, clients have reported that they absolutely cannot close their eyes and relax. In these unusual cases, I suggest either going for a walk in a familiar place or rocking in a rocking chair. Whatever works for you to create trance is fine. As you practice, you will be able to vary where and when you go into trance. Previously,

I mentioned that I can go into trance in practically any setting with a moment's notice.

Sometimes I have students who complain that they fall asleep when they start to practice self-hypnosis. If this happens to you, try doing trance sitting in a chair. Uncross your legs and place your hands on the arms of the chair or on your thighs. This is the best sitting position for self-hypnosis.

In self-hypnosis, you may want to suggest to yourself that improvement will occur. Before you are to come out of trance, say, "The next time I go into trance, it will be even easier and more enjoyable for me to go into trance."

METHODS OF GOING INTO TRANCE

Here are three methods of going into trance. The first, the relaxing-place method, is the one I usually teach to my clients in therapy. The other two methods I teach in classes on self-hypnosis.

METHODS OF SELF-HYPNOSIS

RELAXING-PLACE METHOD
Take three deep breaths
Imagine:
Three sights of the relaxing place
Three feelings of the relaxing place
Three smells of the relaxing place
Three sounds of the relaxing place

MUSCLE-GROUP METHOD
Take three deep breaths
Start with either head or toes
Relax each part of the body

EYE-ROLL METHOD
Roll eyes up
Close lids with eyes rolled up
Take a deep breath
Exhale and relax

Relaxing-Place Method
Begin by taking three deep breaths. As you breathe in, imagine breathing in "peace." As you exhale, imagine breathing out "tension." You

might say, "Breathe in peace; exhale tension."
You might imagine the air going in as being a
soothing blue color, while the tension air might
be red or you might imagine the peaceful air
being cool and the tension air being hot.

You then think of being in a relaxing place.
You might pick the woods, the beach, or sitting
in front of a fireplace. I asked one client what
the most relaxing place would be for him, and
he said the cockpit of a plane. That would not
have been my first choice. It was his, however.
Remember, whatever works for you is fine.

As you imagine the relaxing place, recall
the sights, sounds, smells, and feelings of the
relaxing place. You will see exactly how to do
this in the script on the following pages, but I
encourage you to be creative and flexible in
designing this for yourself.

Once, when I hypnotized a ten-year-old girl,
she said that her grandmother's backyard was
the most relaxing place for her. She described it
generally; then I described it in some detail for
her as she went into trance. I said that she could
notice the interesting patterns the sunlight
makes on the ground as it shines through the
trees and the greenness of the leaves and the
grass (sights). She could notice the clouds
floating lazily in the sky (sights). She could
notice the smell of the earth, the smell of mowed
grass, the smell of any plant in her
grandmother's backyard (smells). She could
hear the sounds of birds, the breeze blowing
through the trees, the sound of a lawn mower off

in the distance (sounds). She could feel the soft breeze blowing on her hair, the warmth of the sun on her face, or the cool dampness of the grass under her body (feelings). (I do not usually do these in a specific order, but make an attempt to include three of each of these categories— sights, sounds, smells, and feelings.) As I said these things, I talked slowly and in a soft, monotone voice. This change in voice tone and speed was not contrived on my part, but a result of having entered into trance with the client.

The following is a script using beach imagery that you might use to go into trance:

Take three deep breaths. As you inhale, say to yourself, "Breathe in peace." As you breathe out, say, "Exhale tension." As you exhale the third time, allow your body to slump. You could allow any outside noises to help you go more deeply into trance, feeling more relaxed and comfortable. You can now imagine being on the beach. You may notice the varied sounds of the waves as they come in with a roar and the soft musical sound as they go out over and over again. You may notice the smell of the salty water as you feel the healing warmth of the sun on your skin. You could look out over the water and notice how the ocean is different colors in different places and how the sunlight dances upon the water. You might notice the smell of your favorite sunscreen and the oily feeling on your skin. You could notice the sounds of birds near the beach and look out over the ocean. You might see a seagull catching the wind in her wings and just remaining lazily suspended in the air. You might notice the sounds of people playing on the beach in the distance or notice the sounds of the wind coming off the ocean. You might reach down and pick up a handful of warm sand and feel the tickling sensation of it flowing between your fingers, noticing how each grain is different. You could notice the moist warmth of the sea breeze as it lightly moves the hair on your body.

You may notice that I tended to use tentative words like *may, might, could,* and *can.* This is a characteristic of brief solution-oriented hypnosis that is very permissive. (If you would like further information about this method, read *Solution-Oriented Hypnosis: An Ericksonian Approach*, by O'Hanlon and Martin, W. W. Norton, 1992. In fact, buy this book. My husband is one of the authors.)

I have emphasized visual images, and often the word "imagery" brings to mind visual experiences. Some people are not as visual as others and respond more to sounds or feelings. If you think of relaxing sounds as being most powerful in inducing a trance for you, focus on sounds and minimize sights. I find the sound of rain very trance-inducing. Some find music very trance-inducing. If you are more auditory than visual in your imagery, you might emphasize the sounds of the breeze in the trees or the sounds of water to get relaxed. If you find that bodily sensations affect you the most, use images of temperature or other physical sensations.

You may have noticed that I tend to use a literary style, instead of just a cold factual description. Again, allow yourself to be creative and make the visual, auditory, olfactory (smells), and tactile images (feelings) as intense as you might like. Generally, I prefer that you make up these scripts as you go. If you need a start, you could initially make an audio tape for yourself by reading the beach imagery found earlier in this chapter into a tape recorder or writing and reading a script of your own into the recorder. Of course, you can also look at the back of this book at the list of my tapes and buy one of mine.

You will find that many parts of this book emphasize visualization. You may wonder how imagery and self-hypnosis differ. Self-hypnosis allows you to be in touch with sensations and feelings as well as thoughts, whereas imagery primarily focuses on thoughts. For some methods of going into trance, imagery is part of the process, but you can go into trance without imagery. Through hypnosis, you can experience being in a situation with a greater intensity than through imagery alone. Finally, information you get from your unconscious through self-hypnosis differs from creating images. In self-hypnosis, you may deliberately ask your unconscious for memories that are not available through imagination alone.

Muscle-Group Method
This is the method I first learned when I was taught self-hypnosis. The muscle-group method is excellent also for relieving physical discomfort or relaxing your body.

You may begin with the same breathing imagery as before, and again suggest that outside noises help you to relax more. The following is an example of what to do after those general suggestions:

Let the tension begin to flow out of your toes. Relax your toes. Relax your feet. Your feet may feel tingly or they may begin to feel warm. Allow that relaxation to flow up your ankles and calves, and then surround your knees. Loosen the muscles in your thighs. Let your legs feel loose, like the legs of a rag doll. Allow that relaxed sensation to flow up your legs to your hips and your genitals. Let that comfort and relaxation fill your hips and your genitals. Let that comfort and relaxation spread to your intestines, your bladder, and your lower back. Allow your stomach and the middle of your back to feel comfortable and loose, just as if you were floating in warm bath water. Let that relaxation spread up your body to your chest and upper back. Notice the relaxation surrounding each vertebra of your spine. Allow relaxation to spread across the back of your shoulders, loosening those muscles and letting them feel soft and comfortable. Relax your chest. Let that relaxed feeling spread down your arms all the way out to your fingertips. Let those arms hang loosely and comfortably from your shoulders, like the tail of a kite. Allow that comfortable relaxed feeling to surround the vertebrae in your neck and loosen the muscles in the back and then the front of your neck. Loosen those facial muscles and allow relaxation to spread throughout your jaw and around the back of your head. Allow that relaxation to fill your cheeks and your sinuses and flow over and around your eyes. Let that comfort and relaxation flow up your forehead and fill your temples, flowing up over your entire scalp. Now continue to breathe in peace and exhale any residual tension.

It is fine to start with your head and work down if that seems more natural for you.

Spiegel's Eye-Roll Method
Herbert and David Spiegel (father and son) have a simple three-step method:
ONE: With you eyes open, roll your eyes up towards your eyebrows as high as you can get them. Try to see the top of your head. TWO: With your eyes still gazing upwards, close your lids and take in a deep breath. THREE: Exhale. Let your eyes relax, and let your body float.

Even though this is not a method that I often use myself, some of my students report that this has become their favorite method. The eye-roll method is a short, simple, and effective method for going into trance.

Now that you have the choice of three popular methods of going into trance, you can plan what to do after you get into trance. Like a new computer consumer sitting at the computer, you have a program in the disk drive and now you need to decide what you are going to do with it.

SUMMARY: Most people experience hypnosis as a relaxed state with focused attention, heightened ability to recall feelings and images, and openness to suggestion. The depth of trance is of only minor importance in determining whether or not you can accomplish your goals. Good subjects are intelligent and motivated and have a good ability to visualize. However, these qualities are not essential to get results in self-hypnosis.

The following three methods for going into trance are recommended:
• creating a relaxing place in your imagination;
• progressively relaxing the muscles of your body; or
• using the Spiegel eye-roll method.

EXERCISE: Practice each of the suggested methods for going into trance and find which is best for you. If reading the instructions and closing your eyes and practicing is not easy for you, make an audio tape of the directions. If you choose to record, read the script from the book slowly, softly, and rhythmically.

CHAPTER 4

MAKING YOUR UNCONSCIOUS USER-FRIENDLY

With computers, the program is user-friendly if it is easy to understand and lets you know what you should do to get the results you want. Learning to communicate with your unconscious with similar ease is the goal of this book. So far, you have learned how to get into a relaxed state where you are most likely to have access to your unconscious. You have also learned to talk to your unconscious. Now you will learn one of the ways to get your unconscious to talk back to you. Your unconscious speaks to you indirectly through dreams and symptoms, but it can directly answer "yes" or "no" questions as well.

GETTING THE DATA

When I first learned to do self-hypnosis in the 1960s, I was trained to signal with my fingers to answer questions asked in trance. I would use the index finger of my right hand to indicate "yes" and the index finger of my left hand for "no." As the years passed, I have continued to be able to ask my unconscious questions and feel a tingling in my finger for the appropriate answer.

In 1978, I attended a workshop on Neuro-Linguistic Programming (NLP), a type of therapy that emphasizes working with the unconscious. The presenters suggested that you let your body choose and generate its own signals for "yes" and "no." In order to do this, you may first wish to put yourself in a light trance. Ask your unconscious to pick some sensation and increase that sensation to indicate a "yes" answer. For me, this is a tingling on the left side of my face. Most of my clients find this to be a tingling in some extremity, such as their hands, but one client experiences "yes" as a throbbing noise in the ears. Just relax and notice which of your sensations increases. Then ask your unconscious to increase it again so you can be sure that it is your "yes" signal. Repeat this procedure for your "no" signal. From time to time, clients will find that their "no" is the clear decrease in their "yes" signal. Be permissive with your unconscious and let it reveal itself in its own favorite way.

Students wonder whether or not their signals will change. I found that my signals changed at first, but now have settled down and have been predictable for several years.

GETTING THE INPUT

What types of questions would you ask your unconscious? You might ask what purpose some behavior or symptom serves. When you use this technique, keep in mind that you cannot know with certainty that the unwanted behavior truly served some underlying purpose, but people often find the motivation to change through this strategy.

Looking for the underlying purpose is a typical method of the type of therapy I mentioned earlier, Neuro-Linguistic Programming (NLP). Therapists using this technique suggest the following steps to explore the purpose of a behavior: Ask your unconscious if it is willing to let your conscious mind know the purpose served by _____ (the symptom or behavior, such as overeating). If it says "yes," then ask it to let you know the purpose now — either through words that come to your mind or through images. If the answer is "no," that really does not pose any difficulty. With a "no" answer, you can still change the problem behavior by adding other ways to serve the unknown purpose without knowing why the behavior was there in the first place.

Sometimes you may feel you know the purpose that something serves. If you have a good guess, ask your unconscious if that symptom or behavior is serving the purpose that you think it does. For example, I have found that having a headache usually is my unconscious mind's way of telling me to take better care of myself. I will put myself into self-hypnosis and then ask if that is the purpose served by this headache. If I get a signal for "yes," then I will ask if taking care of myself would happen by some action, like taking a nap. If the answer is "yes," then I take the action and the headache fades away. If my unconscious indicates that the purpose is not that I need to take care of myself but something else, I will ask my unconscious if it is willing to let me know the purpose.

The underlying concept here is that when we have problems, we are having them because it seems to be the only choice that our unconscious can generate to serve a particular purpose. Even though I maintain a certain skepticism about the validity of the concept that behaviors have an underlying purpose, I have still found it helpful. An example of how this may be used is, if you are depressed, depression might be the only way you can think of to ask for love. If you simply had other choices, then you would no longer be depressed.

In our life experiences, we see people acting in many ways, hear about them doing many different behaviors, and read about alternatives to our usual habits. These possibilities could

range from something as simple as going for a
walk to something as dramatic as moving to
another city. A part of us has access to all these
alternatives and possibilities.

Whether the unconscious lets you know the
purpose the unwanted behavior serves or not, it
can still add ways to serve that known or
unknown purpose. Ask your unconscious to go
to that part of you that has stored all the ways
that might serve this purpose, which we might
call purpose "X." Ask your unconscious to pick
three new ways to serve purpose X, ways that
are just as available and useful as what you are
doing now. Ask your unconscious to give you a
"yes" signal whenever you have a new way to
serve purpose X. Then you can sit quietly and
wait for three "yes" signals. You do not have to
know consciously what these new ways are. Just
notice the "yes" signals. If you are not sure
whether or not you have had three clear "yes"
signals, then ask your unconscious to give you
one clear "yes" if you now have three new
choices. If it says "no," ask it to go back to the
part of you that can generate new or recently
unused actions and pick some more. Again, ask
your unconscious to give you a clear signal
when those new choices are available. If your
unconscious comes up with only two, that is
satisfactory.

On rare occasions I have had a client who
could not come up with alternative ways to serve
purpose X. Then I simply ask the client's
unconscious to work on resolving the barriers to

change while the client is asleep and try again later. This has proven successful.

You want to be sure that the new choices fit with your values. Ask your unconscious if these new choices are acceptable to all parts of you. The point here is to guard against your unconscious choosing another irritating behavior. For example, if for the depressed person the new option were to be sexually promiscuous, the unconscious would likely give you a "no" response to the question, "Are these new choices acceptable to all parts of you?" If you do get a "no," go back one step and ask your unconscious to change whatever is necessary for you to have three new acceptable choices available to you. If you get a "yes," then ask your unconscious to guarantee that it will try out these new ways within the next month.

As I mentioned before, it is not necessary that your conscious mind know what you picked. Usually people are not sure what the new choices will be. Sometimes they may have an idea what they want, but generally they discover the new choices by noticing the new behaviors that they acquire over the next month. Sometimes a client will come back in a week or two and report some dramatic change, such as quitting a job or buying a house. More often they will report some less dramatic change, such as starting to play the piano again, calling an old friend, or writing a journal.

You might want to ask your unconscious other questions: Is this difficulty related to something earlier in my life? If the unconscious answers "yes" and you wish to pursue this, ask your unconscious if this occurred before age 20, 17, 15, etc., until you isolate the age. Then you might ask your unconscious to let you remember the event either at that moment or over the next two weeks. My therapeutic philosophy is that you need not know the origin of difficulties to change your behavior. Knowing when a difficulty started is interesting, even if the knowledge of it is not essential for change.

I was once working with a woman who was a full-time nurse and single parent of two children. She kept referring to herself as "lazy." It seemed to me that she was anything but lazy, and we explored the origin of this label under hypnosis. In trance, she recalled that when she was a teenager her father had screamed at her that she was lazy. She had believed this label ever since and, therefore, frequently referred to herself as lazy. Under hypnosis she agreed to observe how productive she was. After that session she was delighted to discover what an active, energetic person she actually was. She could have spent years in analysis trying to get at this same difficulty, but with hypnosis it took about three sessions.

Perhaps you have a fear that seems to be out of proportion to the actual danger. An example is claustrophobia. You may know when the fear began, such as a time when an older brother or sister locked you in a closet. Ask your unconscious to give you a signal for "yes" if that is when the difficulty began. Then ask your unconscious to change that memory in some way for you. You might experiment by letting a light be on in the closet as you remember the event. You might ask your unconscious to run that memory backwards as though you were watching a video run backwards. You might imagine scaring the person who locked you in the closet to create a different ending to the memory. Perhaps imagine yourself as you are now, hiding in that closet with the younger you and saying something reassuring to the younger you. The point is to change your relationship to this memory by having it altered in some way.

Retrieving the memory of the first time you had a particular fear may not be possible. Then the best procedure is to again ask your unconscious what purpose this fear is serving and find new ways to serve that function. (I have found that most often the purpose is self-protection.)

Another question of interest might be, "Is my unconscious willing to help me make some particular change?" If it responds positively, I would ask it to make that change within a time period, such as a month. If it says "no," then I would ask it to work on the situation while I am sleeping. This usually results in change in the future.

A helpful question could be "Will my unconscious give me some new understanding about some issue?" Assuming that you get a "yes" answer, I would ask it then to do whatever is necessary within some reasonable time period. If it says "no," then I would again ask the unconscious to work on removing the barriers to resolving the difficulty while I am dreaming. (The next chapter gives instructions on how to do this.)

Several years ago I had an experience with a client that deepened my commitment to working with the unconscious. The man I was working with was a commercial artist in his mid-twenties. He was single and in partnership with a single woman in her mid-twenties. He was lonely and very fearful of being touched. He said that no one had touched him in a year, not even his own mother who lived in the same city. He was so afraid of being touched that he would not even go to a busy shopping center for fear that someone might accidentally bump into him. I asked him how he avoided shaking hands in business situations, and he reported several ways to prevent people from shaking your hand.

I put him in a light trance and said that I was sure that avoiding being touched had served some very important purpose for him and that his unconscious mind could come up with some new way of serving that purpose within the next week. I suggested that these new ways would support his self-esteem and health. When he returned the next week, I asked him if anything unusual had happened since our last session. He told me that during the week he was sitting alone with his partner and had started staring at her feet. She had asked what he was doing.

He replied, "I have this urge to give you a foot massage." She said, "Sure." He gave her a foot massage. She gave him a foot massage. He gave her a back rub. She gave him a back rub. He gave her a body massage. She gave him a body massage. This was an almost unbelievable breakthrough for someone who had not been touched or touched anyone for one year. I had always had a positive attitude towards the unconscious, but this experience was so striking that I recommitted myself to using this invaluable resource and to teaching others to do so.

You may have noticed in that case study I never found out why he had been that phobic about being touched, although we had looked for some explanations. The successful change came when the unconscious was asked to make the change.

Some of my students have pointed out to me that asking questions of my own unconscious is easier for me because, being a psychologist, I know what to ask. That is true. I am not suggesting that you can do all your own therapy, but there are times when being able to talk to your unconscious will help you. Certainly, if you are having major problems, seek professional help. I often find that my clients add to the positive effect of therapy by reading self-help books. The techniques in this book can add to the beneficial effects of therapy.

DELETING THE MEMORIES

As I suggested before, you may wish to get some distance from some painful memories by using imagery. Often we have had events in our lives that continue to have a negative influence upon us. These events can intrude upon us through fears haunting our thoughts or, in the case of severe trauma, flashbacks. Fortunately, most of us do not have traumas severe enough to have flashbacks. Flashbacks are stronger than memories. When someone has a flashback, it is as though the event is happening again in the present, like reliving a violent scene such as being raped or mugged. Examples of negative events that might haunt us are discovering your mate has a lover, recalling a physically frightening event such as a car accident, or simply doing a very bad job at something, such as a presentation at work.

A trance technique that I have used with myself and with my clients is to imagine sitting in a movie theater. This is a private showing just for you. Notice the darkness of the lights, how the seat feels beneath you, and maybe even the smell of popcorn from the lobby. Let the scene that you want to forget play before you on the screen. Watch it the same way you would a documentary, not reliving the experience, but just seeing it before you. When it concludes, see the words "THE END" upon the screen.

Connirae and Steve Andreas, NLP therapists in Colorado, use a similar method for treating phobias. Given that you know what traumatic event started the phobia, they suggest running the movie of that event fast backwards and fast forward and then being in the movie fast forward and fast backwards. This seems to eliminate the phobia. You could add this approach to seeing the first run feature of your mental movie.

Imagine that you slowly get out of your seat and go out to the lobby where someone meets you. (This person could be a stranger, a friend, or a spiritual guide.) He or she hands you that reel of film containing all the memories, all the feelings that went with those memories, and all the interference capacities that those memories had for you. Imagine taking that film out to the parking lot of the theater. There you find a roaring bonfire. Smell the smoke, feel the heat, and hear the crackle of the flames. Throw the reel of memories with all its power over you into the fire. Watch the film flash as it burns and watch the metal parts melt into a misshapen metal glob. As the smoke rises, let your negative feelings from the event drift away too. Imagine the person who gave you the reel saying something that will help you feel totally free of the emotional effect that this memory has had over you. Feel the relief.

Some memories are simply too overwhelming to be dealt with without a therapist to help you. I have had clients who have been severely sexually abused as children and clients who have been ritualistically abused by satanic cults. Those memories are not ones that you can deal with by yourself. Find a therapist who is well trained, who knows hypnosis, and who has had experience dealing with people who have suffered in that way.

We have all had unpleasant experiences that we would like to avoid repeating, even mentally. The techniques in this chapter will not erase your memories totally, but can greatly diminish the power and intrusive element that the memories have.

SUMMARY: The unconscious can provide us with signals for "yes" and "no." These signals can be used for asking the unconscious questions and getting it to help in overcoming difficulties. This help can come through asking what purpose a behavior is serving, or what the origin of a difficulty is, and asking your unconscious for a change.

EXERCISE: Pick anything that you want to change. Ask your unconscious if it is willing to let you know the purpose that the behavior serves. You may explore the purpose if your unconscious is willing to tell you. However, the next step is the crucial one. Ask your unconscious to choose three new ways to serve the purpose that the behavior you want to change serves. Remember, you do not consciously have to know what these changes are going to be, just that your unconscious is willing to accept the assignment. Then, if your unconscious agrees to let you have new choices available to you, ask for a guarantee that it will let you try out these ways. Your unconscious will generate changes for you.

CHAPTER 5

PROGRAMMING YOUR DREAMS

At this point, hopefully, you are able to reach your unconscious by going into trance and to get simple yes-no answers from your unconscious. Now we are going to tap into the wonderful unlimited communicative ability of your unconscious: dreaming.

The unconscious communicates with you every night. It works things out for you in your sleep. Nightmares and repetitive dreams are the unconscious's way of trying to give you a message. Learning to listen to my unconscious through my dreams has been almost as valuable to me as hypnosis. Often my unconscious knows more about me and the changes that I am going through than does my conscious mind. Whenever something has occurred of major significance in my life, such as my divorce, my unconscious seemed to have a greater understanding and perspective about the situation much earlier in the process than my conscious mind did.

For some years I had been keeping track of my dreams, attempting to interpret them with some success, and then I read the excellent book by Gayle Delaney, *Living Your Dreams.* Her book suggests that you can ask your unconscious to have a dream about a particular subject. I have applied these techniques for several years with clients, students in dream interpretation groups, and myself. I am going to summarize these techniques for you.

ASKING FOR A FILE

In using a computer, you store information in files. When you wish to get certain information, you retrieve that file. That is very similar to what I am suggesting in asking for a particular dream. You pick the file you want and then retrieve it while you are sleeping.

What types of issues might you want to deal with? You might ask for more understanding about a relationship with someone or for advice about what you should do about a job. You might also ask for your unconscious to work on helping you get over some painful event. These are only suggestions. Any topic that is of enough interest for you to want to work on it is acceptable.

The first thing to do in the dream programming process is to use your conscious mind to deal with the issue. Keep a dream journal. Before you go to sleep at night, write down all you can think of regarding that topic.

For example, you might want help getting over a painful relationship. Write down why you should get over it. Write down what the advantages would be if you did **not** get over it. (There might be some valid reason for not getting over the problem.) Consider what purpose you think it might be serving. In other words, consciously analyze the problem as fully as possible. Often this can be a learning experience in itself.

Devise a "dream request" sentence. In our example it could be, "Help me get over the relationship with _____." As you go to sleep, repeat the request over and over to yourself.

Keep a pencil and your dream notebook by your bed to record your dream as soon as you awaken. It is true that we all dream every night. If you do not write the dream down immediately, the dream seems to automatically erase. I usually remember a couple of dreams from each night's sleep and record only the ones that seem most vivid. My unconscious usually makes it clear which dream is the answer to my request.

Most of the time I am not "working" on anything. I find that if there is something I need to pay attention to, it will reach my consciousness in one of three ways. The first is that I will notice that I feel upset. The second is that I may develop a physical symptom such as a headache. The third is that I will have a vivid dream that will grab my attention. As a follow-up on a vivid dream, I will first analyze the dream. Then, if I need to find out something more, I will program my unconscious to dream about the topic again.

I had a tubal ligation scheduled a month in advance. My unconscious had five dreams about men I had known throughout my life and with whom I had thought I might have a child. Saying "good-bye" to that possibility was one of the steps that I needed to go through. I continued to have dreams that seemed to be about being a woman and what that meant for me. Finally, I found, even though my unconscious said I should go ahead with the surgery, that I still felt some uneasiness. I asked my unconscious to have a dream about anything that might still need to be resolved for me about the surgery. I had a dream about a hypnotherapist who taught a relationship class. That is what my husband and I do together in the waking world. The dream made it clear to me that I needed to have my husband change the way he was talking and acting about the surgery. He had been resisting my efforts to get him to have a vasectomy. Also, he had seemed indifferent to my feeling that this was a grief experience, knowing that I would never bear another child. I asked him to change how he talked to me about this and he did. When I asked, "Is there anything else that I need to work on before surgery?" there was nothing else. I noticed at that point I was looking forward to the freedom the outcome would bring and was over any sadness I had about the tubal ligation.

UNDERSTANDING THE MESSAGE

There are three ways to interpret dreams. The first is to make a guess about what the symbolism is in terms of objects, places, and people in the dream. Ask yourself, "How is the dream like my life?" For example, if you dream about a child, that might be some tender young part of yourself. A client of mine, a single man in his mid-thirties who worked for a feed and grain company, illustrated this. He loved his job to such an extent that he neglected his personal life. He dreamed that some children were touring the plant and a little boy fell into a vat of feed. My client reached in and saved the boy. When we interpreted the dream, my client clearly saw that his unconscious was trying to get him to rescue the little boy within his being and that he needed to change his lifestyle. Over the next few sessions he worked on this. Three years later he dropped by my office. He had significantly changed the balance between work and play and he brought his new wife and baby to see me. Often, of course, the messages may not be that clear.

If you dream about being frustrated with something, then ask yourself what is frustrating you in your life. If you dream about an up-coming event that is stressful, it may be only that your unconscious is encouraging you to be prepared for that event. You are every part of your dream. You are all the characters, all the props, and all the actions.

A second way of interpreting dreams is to act as if you are the things in your dream. For example, if you dream of a bridge, talk as if you are a bridge. "I am a bridge. People depend upon me for support. I have to be strong so they won't fall into the river . . . ." If there is a monster in your dream, then talk as if you are the monster. Start by saying, "I am a monster. I do . . . ." This technique comes from Gestalt therapy and is very useful, particularly for people just beginning to interpret their own dreams.

The third way to interpret dreams is to study the language of the dream. I look for puns and double meanings in dreams. One of my clients joined a dream group that I was leading. She had been enduring a marriage wherein, for three years, her husband continued to be in love with a neighbor. As a student in my dream class, she began to focus on her dreams. She had a clear dream of a flat tire. I suggested that perhaps she was just "flat tired." She laughed and began to accept that her attempts to save the marriage were wasted.

When I awaken in the morning, I will usually discuss my dreams with my husband, Bill O'Hanlon, who is also a therapist. Often, as I relate the content of my dream out loud, the meaning will become clear. A recent example of a pun in my dreams was a dream I had that seemed to be about balancing my roles as a woman and a professional. In the dream I was in a frilly pink "ladies room" on a ship. There was a rough, troubled sea outside the porthole. I interpreted this to mean that relying on traditional femininity was dangerous. The ship safely arrived at the dock and then I found it difficult to get off the ship because there was so much equipment on the dock that I could not really get to the shore. The pink ladies room was not safe, but I could get stuck working too much, that is, being a "doc." The pun of the dock was to alert me to the danger of overwork in my career.

Four things are helpful in interpreting your dreams: reading about dream interpretation, joining a dream interpretation group, discussing your dreams with a friend (because the process of relating them out loud is important), and writing them down. In your dream notebook I suggest that you leave a wide margin next to your recorded dream so that you can make notes about what interpretations you have. The process of writing itself will help you get some perspective about the dream, as well as help you accurately remember dreams.

On rare occasions I have had dreams that warned me of trouble ahead. I had been married for thirteen years when, three years before my divorce, I dreamed vividly that a revolution was coming. In the dream I got on a bus that, after a long journey, took me to a therapist's office. I used the dream as a warning to get into therapy before it was too late. As it turned out, the therapy did not save the marriage. It did help the transition beyond the marriage so that the divorce could be more peaceful.

I do think clairvoyant dreams are possible. I have had minor ones, such as dreaming about a flood near my parents' apartment only to awaken to the news that there had been a flood near my parents' apartment. I have a friend who dreamed three times that the man she was about to marry was going to die. After she married him, he became terminally ill. Then she dreamed that the funeral would be on their wedding anniversary. After his long illness, the funeral was on their anniversary.

I tend to expect most dreams to be of the "working on something" garden variety, but there are exceptions. I had a single, male therapist friend who had a vivid dream about a flute player being the woman for him. He awoke from the dream and then went back to sleep asking his unconscious how he could meet her. His unconscious said talk to Janet, a friend of his who played in the symphony. The therapist and the woman who plays flute in the symphony dated for two years and have been married now for three years.

GIVING CREATIVE ASSIGNMENTS TO
YOUR UNCONSCIOUS

As I suggested before, whenever I have a creative endeavor to perform, such as writing this book or giving a speech, I will ask my unconscious to work on it. When I go to bed I will look at my outline or the articles and ideas that I have gathered on the topic and then ask my unconscious to organize it for me while I sleep. Or, if I have been stuck about a particular case I am working on, I will ask my unconscious to come up with a new approach. I will usually wake up with a clear plan in my head, and the information for the project seems to flow easily.

If you have an artistic project, ask your unconscious to work on it while you sleep, particularly if you feel blocked. Present to your unconscious your artistic goal, such as a song that has been brewing in your mind. Upon awakening, you may find the creative blocks that you had have crumbled.

If you have some material that you need to organize from your work or home life, such as redecorating your house or thinking of a clever present for someone special, ask your unconscious to work on it for you. You may be pleasantly surprised with the ideas that your unconscious generates for you. There have been times when I have asked my unconscious to help me find a way to express my love for my husband or one of my children. Sometimes the answer will be clear in a dream, and sometimes I will simply notice there is no longer a block to being close to that family member.

SUMMARY: Your unconscious will help you focus on issues and generate solutions for problems given to it. You can program your unconscious mind to have a dream by having it focus upon a particular issue you wish to explore. Dream interpretation happens through looking for symbolism, for puns, and for directives.

EXERCISE: Ask your unconscious to help you pick out an issue to change. Write down the positives and negatives of getting over this problem. Pick a sentence that represents the help you want from your unconscious to repeat as you go to sleep. Repeat this request over and over as you fall asleep. As soon as you awaken, write down your dream.

When you explore interpreting that dream use these three methods:
• Talk or write as if you are all parts of the dream.
• Write down what overall themes are in the dream.
• Notice any puns or words with double meanings that happen in the dream.

Find someone who also wants to explore dreams, and meet with that person once a week to go over dreams.

CHAPTER 6

GETTING OUT OF THE HABIT

The purpose of this chapter is to help you use your unconscious to change actions. Often we want to stop actions that are a problem to us in terms of self-esteem. These problems might be weight control, nail biting, or a life-threatening problem, such as smoking.

HABIT CONTROL

With my clients I have found a large number of techniques that are effective in changing habits. These include acting differently around the habit, resisting the impulse to resume the habit, using negative and positive imagery, and using self-hypnosis.

By doing something different concerning the action of the habit you can loosen the grip of the habit before you use self-hypnosis. For example, if the habit is smoking, you may first want to do what is called *forced smoking*.

Forced smoking is inhaling from the cigarette every 12 seconds, instead of the usual leisurely smoking. Smokers are instructed to continue taking drags until they feel uncomfortable and to smoke only in that manner for a week. In addition, they are to smoke in settings that are not their usual comfortable smoking places. The idea is to bring the habit out of the unconscious, automatic arena into awareness.

There are also ways of doing something different around eating habits. For example, if you have difficulties with eating too much chocolate, I suggest eating all the chocolate you want but only in the bathroom, with your clothes off, looking in the mirror. If you are firmly committed to changing your habits, and take actions, often you do not need hypnosis, probably because most habits can be controlled through conscious effort. Generally, the rule is for you to make no exceptions to the habit you are changing. If food is a problem and you find yourself saying, "I'll just have this little hot fudge sundae," making this exception tends to undermine your sense of accomplishment and opens the way for more exceptions.

A couple of temporary alterations can help you get through the first few days of changing a habit. If you want to change a negative habit, such as overeating or smoking, during the time that you are making these changes, eliminate liquor and caffeine. Alcohol tends to undermine resolve when you are changing habits, and caffeine tends to make you tense so that you feel the need for the tranquilizing effect of cigarettes or food.

A final word about habit changes is that all of us have a part of ourselves that wants *what* it wants *when* it wants it. This is our child part. The little child that we once were is still in each of us, and we may have to deal with him or her in a parental way. If you have children, you may recall during their preschool years having nightly bedtime battles. They wanted to stay up and play and would cry when you put them to bed. If you were firm and did not go get them, they might have cried the first day for a while. The second day they might have cried less, and by the third day they probably did not complain at all. Sometimes we need to approach ourselves with that same firmness. Nothing awful will happen to you if you do not get to do what you want to, when you want to. You may fear that if you try to quit smoking, you might have a nervous breakdown or gain weight and become the size of a house. These awful things do not have to happen. However, if you don't stop, there is significant medical evidence that something awful is likely to happen to you. If the habit you are changing is adding exercise to your life, it may seem as if you are taking a reluctant child to the dentist to get yourself to exercise at first. Not letting your mood determine your actions is an important part of change.

USING THE IMAGERY OF SELF-HYPNOSIS TO CHANGE HABITS

When something is as important as quitting smoking, you might want to use fear-producing imagery. I had a client whose mother died of emphysema. I suggested to him that each time he heard the word "cigarette," smelled cigarette smoke, touched a cigarette, or thought of cigarettes, he would remember what his mother had been like in the last few months of her life. He successfully quit smoking, and I think that this image helped. There may be someone you have cared for or met who had lung cancer or emphysema. Your unconscious could associate that person's memory and image with the sight, smell, or thought of smoking. Making the connection between the action and the potential result is the turning point for many clients.

Dr. Herbert Spiegel, the psychiatrist, suggests that you repeat a phrase reminding yourself of the magnitude of the danger. *"I need my body to live. Cigarettes are poison to my body; therefore for my body, I will not smoke. I am my body's keeper."*

Food, I am happy to report, is not usually poison, so such drastic self-sentences are not necessary to get the results you may want. For both food and cigarettes, however, the loss of self-control often comes at times when you feel tense. To avoid letting tension interfere with your goal, say to yourself, when in trance, *"Whenever I see*

_____ *(a cigarette or food), hear* _____ *(food words, or the word "cigarette"), smell* _____ *(a cigarette or food), or think of* _____ *(a cigarette or food), that will be the signal for me to relax, breathing deeply, inhaling peace and exhaling tension."* The point is to do something to relieve the tension besides resorting to your habit.

This type of suggestion can be used in a positive way with food. For example, bring to your mind the image of exactly how you would like to look. Imagine how your body would feel. Let this picture and the sensations with it be very vivid. Whenever you see, smell, hear, touch, or taste food, you can let this vision of exactly how you would like to look determine how much and what you put in your mouth. One of my clients had such a strong positive reaction to this that even on a coffee break at work she would get a vivid image of her goal just from looking at a donut.

My father, Dr. Lofton Hudson, who has been doing hypnotherapy since the 1950s, has people who want to lose weight rename their favorite fattening goodies "cat food" or "dog food" and then imagine themselves being revolted by the goodies. After renaming the food, when they see a television ad for those products, their mouth seldom waters.

I find it helpful to remind myself of the report several years ago about the amount of rat hairs and feces that were allowed in chocolate. Envisioning rat hairs and feces also prevents my mouth from watering. Either strong negative images or positive pleasurable images can provide motivation.

Images can help you to avoid temptation and to improve motivation. Let the image of what you will be like when you have accomplished your habit goal pull you through the rough times by simply closing your eyes and focusing on having become a non-smoker or a person with a healthy weight. Let how you would *feel* physically and emotionally be clear to you. Let how you would *look* be clear to you. Once a day, when you are practicing your self-hypnosis, let those images become very vivid for you. Just thinking of this once a day or more could in itself be very useful to you.

In follow-up studies of smoking cessation programs, the researchers found that those who returned to smoking did so in certain settings. Home was the most common, work next, and then social situations. Often, clients will tell me they fear that they will return to smoking when they are out drinking with friends. I have them visualize the situation they fear will be most likely to cause them trouble and imagine themselves resisting smoking and feeling wonderful about doing so. If you anticipate a particular situation that may be a difficult one in maintaining your changed habit, then imagine that situation with you successfully avoiding the habit. It also may be advisable to avoid alcohol for a month or so while you are building your confidence in your newly changed self.

One of the major difficulties for overweight people is that they do not stop eating when they are full, but continue to eat, ignoring their internal cues telling them when they are full. I have found some clients have success with asking their unconscious to produce a sensation of coolness instead of fullness when they have had an adequate amount to eat. I have also suggested to them in trance that, when they are approaching the point of just adequate fullness, they will notice that food begins to lose its taste and becomes less interesting and satisfying.

Many hypnotherapists recommend having a "will binder" for negative habits such as smoking. A will binder is a statement like: *"I would no more have a cigarette, than _____ (I would rob a gas station, shoot my child, pick my nose before an audience, etc.)."* Pick (or perhaps "choose" would be a better choice of words) something that would be completely out of the question. You may want to put yourself into trance and ask your unconscious to generate a will binder that will come to your mind whenever you think of repeating the habit you want to avoid.

One habit that I have helped many people change is nail biting. Besides imagining fingernails being the desired length, I include two other suggestions. Whenever the hand starts to move towards the mouth, it will feel heavy. In this suggestion, the heaviness can be below your level of awareness or you can arrange to notice it. The second suggestion is that instead of biting the nails you can caress your nails with your thumb.

You might practice caressing your nails while you are in trance.

As with the other habits, a conscious change will make a difference, too. A man I know changed his nail biting habit by biting only his little fingernail. Whenever he would begin to bite his nails, he would say to himself, "No, you can bite all you want on this one nail, but you leave the other nails alone." Eventually he gave up biting that fingernail, too. While doing this consciously would probably be sufficient to change the habit, doing this in trance would make it even easier because having the help of your unconscious gets all parts of you working together.

CHANGING HABITS

Do the habit differently
(Smoke in an unusual way; eat in an odd place)

Keep the adult part of you in charge

Imagine having succeeded

Use negative images of what would happen
if the habit were not changed

Create a will binder: "I would no more
smoke a cigarette, than I would . . . ."

Another image to use in self-hypnosis that can help change a habit is to fantasize that it is a year from now, with your goal reached and secure. Imagine someone who cares very much for you, like your parents, a spouse, or a friend. Without a specific person in your life now, you could imagine either a deceased grandparent or a religious being. Picture them being thrilled with your success, congratulating you, and perhaps giving you a hug. Feel the joy and pride that you would feel in that context. Ask your unconscious to help you move towards that goal.

Finally, in trance ask your unconscious to do whatever is necessary to help you change this habit. We will discuss finding out what purpose the habit might be serving in a later chapter. Sometimes, however, a general request for help from your unconscious may be all that is necessary. Say to your unconscious, "Consciously, I do not know what changes may need to occur internally. There may be memories that I could see in a new way or new understandings that I need to have. But whatever needs to happen to bring about this change, I ask that you, unconscious mind, begin to make those alterations. These changes may be as small as distracting my attention, or as big as suddenly remembering a major upsetting event. I ask you to quickly make whatever changes are necessary to support this change in a way that will be appropriate."

SUMMARY: Both conscious and unconscious techniques can be combined to change habits. Consciously, you can do something different around the habit as a preparation for changing and make choices that will support that change. You can enlist the help of your unconscious through self-hypnosis and imagery, imagining success in the future, helping yourself relax around the habit you want to change, using a will binder, and generally asking for support from your unconscious in making changes.

EXERCISE: Make some notes about what you would like to accomplish during hypnosis: the image of how you would like to look or feel, what it will be like when you succeed in changing your habit, relaxing in the presence of the temptation, what may happen to you if you do not change your habit, and/or a will binder, if the habit is something that you want to eliminate completely. Put yourself in trance and use these images to succeed in making the changes you need to make in your habit. Practice self-hypnosis daily, reinforcing these images and your commitment to change.

CHAPTER 7

DELETING FEAR AND PERFORMING YOUR BEST

Whenever I conduct assertiveness training classes, I include learning to relax and the use of imagery. One of the books I read on assertiveness contained a wonderful cartoon. A woman was sitting at a desk with a placid look on her face. Over her head in a "thought bubble" was a picture of her lying on the beach sunbathing. A man, looking irate, was pounding on her desk, apparently yelling at her. This idea, the ability to focus on a relaxing image in a stress-producing situation, is an excellent resource for you. Besides, it could make it less likely anyone will be pounding on your desk in the first place.

SYSTEMATIC DESENSITIZATION

A psychotherapeutic technique that has proven successful in treating phobias is Systematic Desensitization. Joseph Wolpe, a psychiatrist, developed this technique. He has patients make a list of increasingly fear-provoking situations. For example, if airplanes frighten you, your list might include: going to the airport, parking your car, checking in at the counter, going to the gate, getting on the plane, fastening the seat belt, hearing the engine start, etc. Wolpe teaches his clients to become proficient at relaxation. Then the client is to start with the least fear-provoking image and switch back and forth between the relaxing image and the fear-producing image until the patient can remain relaxed when thinking of that fear-producing image. Each higher level of fear-producing image is then mastered by this switch technique until the person is able to imagine and then finally perform the desired behavior without the physical sensations associated with fear. The underlying idea is that fear and relaxation are incompatible responses. By becoming proficient at relaxing in the previously fear-producing setting, the client eliminates the phobia.

FIGHTING THE FEAR WITH YOUR UNCONSCIOUS

Another way in which you might use self-hypnosis is to go into trance in the fear-producing situation. This is not difficult if you are not required to do anything more than to be there, as on a plane or on a cart in a pre-operation setting. If you must be doing something, then more practice will be necessary to maintain the relaxed state. For example, in a situation requiring more performance, such as giving a speech, you can imagine yourself successfully performing the speech. Rehearse your behavior. Imagine your body maintaining the same relaxed comfort that it has when you are imagining your relaxing place.

On a television show recently, I was interviewed live (no chance to clean up the bloopers). Although I felt some anxiety, I came across very relaxed and confident. Before going on the air, I imagined my relaxing place and breathed in a way consistent with it. When the interview began, I made a point of keeping my muscles as loose as possible.

The point of becoming relaxed is that it is impossible to have two opposite responses simultaneously. You cannot be tense and be having the physiological equivalent of being relaxed (slow breathing and reduced heart rate).

In treating sexual dysfunction, this principle holds. Being anxious and being sexually turned on at the same time is nearly impossible. If a person is not able to perform sexually, then the therapist will typically assign that the client's partner to stimulate the client without a demand to perform. For example, the couple will be instructed to do body massages, but to have no intercourse or touching of breasts or genitals. When the couple learns to relax and enjoy the stimulation, their natural responses usually take over and the difficulty goes away.

Meanwhile, as a secondary benefit, they will be practicing showing affection and enjoying sex by foreplay methods rather than penetration. These techniques are standard procedures suggested by sex therapists Kaplan and Masters and Johnson.

With all this emphasis on relaxation, many people ask whether there is any difference between self-hypnosis and relaxation. I see relaxation as a part of hypnosis. Relaxation is getting there, and self-hypnosis is what you do after you get there. Relaxed bodily sensations can be associated with no concentration, as in the mind clearing of meditation, or with concentration as in self-hypnosis and imagery. Being relaxed is a healthy, helpful response and is very powerful in handling fear and tension. Self-hypnosis can facilitate relaxation happening when and where you need it. In fact, relaxation is part of going into a trance.

When working on a fear-provoking situation, I ask my unconscious, "Do whatever is necessary to help me eliminate the difficulty. If I need to have a memory and see it in a new light or make some change in my way of thinking about an issue, let that happen either consciously or unconsciously." This is an example of how self-hypnosis goes a step further than relaxation by generally tapping into those natural resources of the unconscious.

DO IT ANYWAY

The ultimate way to alter your reaction to a fear-producing situation is to just do it. I was fearful about making speeches twelve years ago. I used my self-hypnosis and relaxation techniques to begin helping myself speak in public and then made myself accept all speech invitations. Eventually, I started a daily call-in talk show on the radio. Just doing it no matter how afraid I felt helped me.

I have suggested to clients who have fear of public speaking that they join a speech-making club, such as Toastmasters, to practice. You can relax all you want, but if you do not ultimately face what you are afraid of, then the fear might still be in charge of you. The way to eliminate these difficulties is to master relaxation, ask your unconscious for help, and **do** what it is that you are afraid to do. Just like the little child within us in the habit example, there is the part of us that yells, "I don't want to. You can't make me." To be able to change phobias, you need to say firmly to that part of yourself, "You can go on **feeling** afraid, but you have to **do** the thing you have been afraid to do."

Feelings and actions are different. You can have the feeling of being angry or afraid, but you can choose what to do about it. Your feelings do not have to cause you to do anything. For example, you can be angry at people and choose to hit a wall, write them a letter, be silent, yell at them, or leave for an hour. You can feel the way you feel and then choose to do something new with your behavior. Fortunately, humans are not robots. Relaxation and self-hypnosis can help you in doing something you were afraid to do or wish to do more easily, but the ultimate success lies in actually doing it.

OVERCOMING FEAR

Put yourself in trance

Imagine a relaxing place

Switch back and forth between
the relaxing place and the fear image

Change how you breathe in the fearful situation

Feel the fear and do it anyway

BEING AS GOOD AS YOU CAN BE

Anyone who has mastered the skills involved in a sport knows that concentration is an important aid in performing your best. However, concentration seems to work best when it happens spontaneously and is not forced. That is the moment when the unconscious takes over for us. Athletes know this. One strategy that can throw off your opponent's tennis game, for instance, is to ask, "How are you playing so well today?" Moving from the unconscious to the conscious realm can disable the opponent.

I have worked with gymnasts and tennis competitors and had some clear success at improving their competitive performances. The strategy that I have used with them is to have them imagine, in detail, playing a perfect game or doing a perfect routine to see themselves succeeding. Then I ask their unconscious minds to help them do that in their next game or routine.

Some strategies are especially effective in enhancing sports performance. First, I would ask the unconscious to reveal whether or not there are any blocks to success. The yes-no techniques you learned earlier would be a good place to start. Ask for some change if it is needed. Second, if being intimidated by a certain opponent is the difficulty, then imagine defeating that person. Ask yourself to remember a time when you thought that you would be defeated by another opponent and were not. Usually, there is some time that each of us has had this experience, but if not, you can imagine such an experience.

Generally, the principle you can use in improving performance is to go into trance and imagine success, asking your unconscious to do the work for you. Most good performers in music, sports, or dance go into a spontaneous trance when they perform. Once I learned this,

I began to observe various performers. Musicians particularly seem unaware of anything but the music. Sometimes they make rather odd faces, and sometimes they have a glazed look in their eyes. Frequently, their facial muscles become smooth as they get into their performance. All of these phenomena are typical of trance.

Assisting and amplifying these natural hypnotic responses can improve the performance. You can do this first by practicing self-hypnosis. Imagine every minute detail of the performance going perfectly—every movement, every breath, every sound involved. Then tell yourself that the signal to begin concentration will be the sight of the golf ball, the net at the tennis court, the keyboard, the podium, or whatever is involved in the activity. Practice this daily for a couple of weeks. When it is almost time for the performance to begin, take a deep breath and relax. Your unconscious will do the rest. Getting your conscious mind out of the way is your biggest task.

MASTERING PERFORMANCE

Imagine doing the task perfectly

If it is a competition, imagine
beating your opponent

Remind yourself that your unconscious
can do it for you

Have an object that is part of the environment
where the performance will occur be
a signal to begin concentrating

SUMMARY: The unconscious and the imagination together can be very helpful in changing actions. We can use those abilities to do things that we have been afraid to do and to improve our performance in some area, such as sports. The overall principle is to imagine success, relax, and get the conscious mind out of our way by going into trance. While the unconscious mind is important, the conscious mind deserves credit too. Conscious choice is the foundation on which change is built. The unconscious, through relaxation and imagery, makes the building easier.

EXERCISE: Pick any performance task that you have wanted to improve, or that you have been afraid to do, such as asking for your money back when dissatisfied with a purchase. First, get yourself into a relaxed state, as you learned in Chapter Two. Imagine the details of doing the task that you want to do successfully. Go into great detail, using all the sights, sounds, and smells of the situation and imagining perfect success. Repeat this process over a few days. (Practice improves any performance, even if the practice is only in your imagination.) Give your unconscious a signal for going into trance, such as the sight of the cash register at the store. Ask your unconscious to help you. Then go do the action. Just before you begin, take a deep breath or two and then let your unconscious do its job.

CHAPTER 8

WHEN YOUR DISK HAS SLIPPED

Fortunately, a disk in the computer cannot slip like the disks in your spine. If you do have pain, the unconscious can be an invaluable resource. The unconscious can provide two services in helping you with physical symptoms. The first is pain management. In this chapter, you will learn several ways to accomplish that. The second service that the unconscious can provide is to promote healing through the use of healing imagery. Examples of this imagery will also be provided in this chapter. I never recommend that skills from your unconscious be a substitute for medical intervention, but those skills can add to the other treatment. Caution is the safest route when the results could have serious consequences. With my clients, I usually work in conjunction with a physician to augment treatment.

Pain can be an important signal from your body telling you that you need to take some sort of action. Those actions may be as minor as drinking less caffeine, or it may be as major as having x-rays to search for a tumor. When I have treated people recovering from a physical trauma, such as a broken bone, I suggest that they will have only the amount of pain that they need to have in order to know how much stress to put on the affected area. Always use the phrase "unnecessary pain" to tell your unconscious what to eliminate. If you become proficient at eliminating pain, you want to leave enough discomfort to know when you are interfering with healing by pushing your body too far.

Many times we have discomfort that does not warrant medical treatment or where medical treatment has already accomplished all it can. At such times as these you might find that controlling the symptom is the best you can do.

For example, I worked with a client who had her femur (thigh bone) broken in a car accident. The bone had to be pinned, and she experienced a great deal of discomfort. She came to me to learn how to hypnotize herself to promote healing and to relieve the pain during her long recovery period. Before she came to me, her orthopedic surgeon recommended additional surgery if the healing did not progress. Through hypnosis and self-hypnosis, she was able to heal quickly, avoiding extra surgery, and manage the pain during recovery. The way she described the change in the pain was that she achieved a different relationship to pain. Although some discomfort was there, it just seemed much less important to her and ceased interfering with her life as it had before.

MANAGING PAIN

Methods for controlling pain are listed with instructions for you to give yourself while you are in trance.

Relaxation

Relaxation itself tends to promote healing and relieve pain. Remember a time when you had discomfort of some sort. You may have let go of the extra tension and it seemed to hurt less. If you become fairly proficient at creating a relaxing place, then you can bring about that relaxation to both relieve and avoid discomfort.

Tension itself can result in pain. You may have noticed in some stressful situations you eventually developed some physical discomfort, such as a headache or stomachache. If you can become sensitive to your body's cues of too much tension, then you may be able to circumvent the pain by using trance just to relax.

There was an interesting study reported by Janus at Yale that dealt with the patients' levels of anxiety before surgery and their recoveries after surgery. The pre-surgery anxiety levels were divided into three categories—high, medium, and low. The high-anxiety people thought that they might die and were sure that they would be in horrible pain following surgery.

The medium-anxiety people anticipated some discomfort but felt that they could manage it. The low-anxiety group expected no difficulty at all, and said they would be back on their feet right away. In terms of actual recovery from the surgery, the medium-anxiety group recovered the fastest.

The point for students of self-hypnosis is that you can have symptom relief from trance, but do not say unrealistic things to yourself, such as I will have no pain at all. (This is good stuff, but there are limits.) I have helped clients with pain management immediately after surgery, and there is no question that they had less pain as soon as they got into trance. Some were able to not have any pain medications after the first day, and others were able to have pain medications less frequently or at a lower dose than was expected.

Dissociation

Dissociation in the case of self-hypnosis has two meanings. The first is taking a view of the situation almost as if it were not happening to you. One of the therapists on my staff had to have extensive oral surgery. The way he managed the discomfort of the surgery was to put himself into trance and then imagine himself standing and watching the surgery as if he were studying the procedure.

I think this is something we can naturally do. I recall having stitches in my finger and taking a "clinical observer" attitude.

Dissociating from an experience as if it were not personal can help avoid some of the discomfort. The opposite would, of course, also be true. If I were sitting in the emergency room thinking, "My God! That's my finger! What are they doing to my finger?" the chances are that I would experience much more pain. Ask your unconscious to help you imagine you are a medical student observing the procedure.

Another way of dissociating yourself from the discomfort is to simply imagine being somewhere else. In the dentist's office, when I was having a cap put on a molar, I went into trance and visualized having a wonderful picnic with my husband and children. I thought of what delicacies we might eat. I imagined the songs we might sing, the jokes we might tell, how the environment would look and feel, and the interesting conversations we could have about the meaning of life.

When I was in labor, about to give birth to my fourth child, my husband kept talking about taking our new baby to a favorite spot in Hawaii. It might be easier, rather than creating a place to go, for you to remember some wonderful time you have already had, perhaps on a vacation. Focusing your attention upon pleasant memories or creating a new fantasy can separate you from the situation and help relieve the discomfort.

Distraction

You may recall some time when you had a headache or a stomachache and got busy doing something, totally forgetting the headache. You might have gone to a movie, gotten into a conversation with a friend, or simply gotten busy with a work project. Again, this is something that we naturally do that you can ask your unconscious to do for you.

I was sitting next to a woman from Finland on a plane when she suddenly felt sick. We had not said much to each other, but after I helped her get the flight attendant, I started talking to her about my visit to Finland—the beautiful woods, how clean the air felt, and other pleasant memories of Finland. (I skipped the part about the great seafood.) She was quickly distracted and was fine by the time we landed.

To use this technique yourself, put yourself in trance and say, "I know I have the ability to distract myself in some way. My unconscious mind may arrange for me to get involved with something and have me be surprised at how quickly the time passes."

If you know of something uncomfortable that you are going to have to do, then you might ask your unconscious to create that specific distraction for you. For example, if you are reading an intriguing novel, you might ask your unconscious to let a couple of pleasant comfortable hours pass with you totally involved in the novel. You do not have to say "and not notice the pain." Your unconscious tends to work best with positive suggestions like, "You will be pleasantly surprised at how much you enjoy . . . ," not negative "don't" suggestions.

My husband and I take a trip every year to celebrate our wedding anniversary. We take turns planning the trip, and five years ago it was my turn to plan. On the recommendation of a relative, I selected an island in the Bahamas called Exuma. In retrospect, the name has an ominous ring to it. During the first two days of our vacation, we lounged leisurely on the beach. On the third day we rented a moped to explore the island. Big mistake! When we rented the moped, the man in charge told us we needed gasoline and that we needed to be sure to get some soon. It was Sunday and we missed the gas station in the town. After exploring the beautiful beaches, we stopped at a country store and inquired about the nearest gas station. The owner said that the one in town was closing in 30 minutes and we needed to move right along to get some gas before it closed. In our haste, we wiped out on a sandy turn, badly gashing the right sides of our bodies. The medical service was very limited, and we did not have access to any significant painkillers. For the next two days, while we were waiting to be well enough to return home, we took turns putting each other in trance and reading a fascinating novel to each other. The novel was an alternative form of trance, and both the direct and indirect methods kept us distracted between the seemingly endless journeys of hobbling to the restaurant and visiting the clinic for bandage changes.

Time Distortion

Another natural phenomenon that you can remind your unconscious to use is time distortion. Perhaps you have had times in your life when minutes seemed to drag by or occasions when time seemed to fly by with great speed. Time itself did not change, but your perception of time did.

Ask your unconscious to let the time when you feel comfortable and most healthy seem to expand — the way it does, for example, when you are waiting for someone. Ask your unconscious to allow the times of discomfort to fly by quickly. You can also ask your unconscious to let you be pleasantly surprised at just how quickly the hours of discomfort pass. This would also be a useful suggestion if you had a hospital experience that you needed to get through. You could say to yourself that while you are in the hospital, time will seem to pass very quickly as it does when you are having a pleasant vacation. You might also tell yourself to be particularly absorbed by an activity in the hospital such as reading or watching television. You might ask your unconscious to plan and imagine the perfect island vacation. All these time distortion suggestions could be combined with the usual pain control suggestions that directly deal with the pain.

Anesthesia
Most adults in our culture have had the experience of being given anesthetic for their dental work or minor surgery. You may remember the sensation of having a part of your body be anesthetized. Another memory might be having your hand in ice water, which is at first painful and then numbing. The point is that your body knows the experience of numbness, if by no other way than having your foot "go to sleep." Your unconscious can re-create this experience for you.

If you happen to know in advance that some area is likely to have discomfort, then you can practice, while in trance, having that part of your body be anesthetized. Some hypnotherapists have you imagine your hand being numb ("glove anesthesia") and have you transfer that experience. The transfer is made by having the sensation move up from your hand to your arm and then to the affected area, or you can place your hand on the affected area after you have succeeded in creating the anesthetic experience in your hand.

I have experimented with glove anesthesia under self-hypnosis. I put myself into a light trance and concentrated on making my hand numb. I experienced my hand feeling different, but I doubted that it was anesthetized. I decided to test this by having my other hand pinch my supposedly anesthetized one. I was surprised that I did not experience the pinch as pain. I could feel the pressure, but not the discomfort.

One of my clients took this image one step further. As I talked to him about imagining anesthetic spreading over the painful area, he imagined painting out the pain with anesthetic. Stroke by stroke, the pain disappeared. I have experimented with both imagining the affected area having the anesthetic experience and with transferring the glove anesthesia and have found both to be effective for me and for my patients.

The Control Center
Using the image of going into the part of the brain that perceives pain and switching off the receptors can be an effective pain control method. Put yourself in trance. Visualize the brain as a major control center, like a boiler room or a computer center. Imagine the sounds of the control center and the knobs that control various areas of your body. If, for example, you are experiencing discomfort in your tooth, you might picture finding the "tooth" knob (like a dimmer switch for a light fixture) and simply turning the knob down. If you are more oriented towards sounds, you could hear a buzzing sound being turned down. Again, the richer and more creative the imagery, the more success and fun you will have. You can imagine little pulses coming from the affected area and those pulses becoming more and more diminished. (If you are an enthusiastic sci-fi movie fan, this should be easy.) The pulses can be lights, noises, or the moving of an indicator needle on the control

panel. Emphasize that your unconscious can eliminate any unnecessary pain.

Sensation Change

In trance, you may ask your unconscious to change the sensation from one of pain to one of coolness, warmth, or pressure. This is particularly important if, for some reason, you need to be aware of how far you are pushing your body. In modifying the sensation you might make analogies. For example, if you want to create a cold sensation, you might remind yourself of making snow balls. You might change a burning sensation to one of pressure, imagining that someone is pressing a cool washcloth on the burning area. In childbirth, imagining pressure instead of pain is a fairly easy transition because there is much pressure. "Pressure" is more comfortable and tolerable than "pain."

HEADACHE PAIN

All of the images above are useful for headache pain, but there are some images that are especially helpful. These images are the same type of images that biofeedback therapists use. The difference between hypnosis and biofeedback is that, in biofeedback, you are hooked up to a machine to monitor your progress. In biofeedback, monitors tell you that you are decreasing various measures of stress responses, such as the temperature of your hands.

With migraines, often the body is experiencing problems in blood circulation. An image that is helpful in changing the flow of blood is that of warming cold hands. In trance, imagine a time when you were warming your hands by a fire, remember having your hands in warm dishwater, and remember the feeling of mittens on your hands. It is even a good idea to actually warm your hands directly.

In one case, I helped a woman eliminate migraines by encouraging her in trance to warm each finger separately. I would start with the little finger of the left hand and have her warm the tip and then have the sensation spread slowly up that finger and all the way up to the wrist. I continued with each finger until we reached the little finger of the right hand. She found this very helpful. You might want to experiment with this method if you have headaches.

With most tension headaches, the problem is a lack of blood flow to the head, followed by too much blood flow to the head. When I was in college, I would drink large amounts of caffeine and be very tense during finals week. After finals, I would often have a headache because of both the caffeine withdrawal and the sudden relaxation of tension. (This made celebrating a problem.) The warming images could have helped in changing the circulation to a less extreme change, thereby decreasing the pain.

(Unfortunately I did not learn this technique until many years after college.)

Another image you can use deals directly with blood flow. Since headaches are often a result of a blood flow changing from constriction of the blood vessels (lack of blood flow) followed by rapid dilation of the blood vessels (excess of blood flow), habitual relaxation can help. To modify chronic ongoing headaches, you can put yourself in hypnosis on a daily basis and say to your unconscious, "You know what is the necessary amount of blood flow to keep my head comfortable. Let those blood vessels in my head be opened for just the correct amount of blood flow for comfort." Prevention can be an excellent treatment for headaches. If you practice relaxation on a daily basis, you're likely to reduce and probably eliminate tension headaches.

PREMENSTRUAL SYNDROME

I have had three clients who came to me wanting treatment for both the psychological upset and physical symptoms associated with Premenstrual Syndrome, PMS. All of these clients received relief from their symptoms for at least six months (my last point of contact with them).

In reporting treatments for PMS, many doctors suggest the elimination of chocolate, caffeine, and salty foods and the use of B vitamins. A treatment method used in England uses suppositories of progesterone, the hormone secreted by the ovaries, but this method has not been practiced on a large scale in the United States. During pregnancy, large amounts of this hormone are in a woman's body. The thought occurred to me to have my clients imagine in trance their ovaries producing progesterone and teach them self-hypnosis so that they could continue the imagery at home. If they had no idea what an ovary looked like, I had them look at an anatomy book and become familiar with the structure. The ovary, which has a bumpy round shape, secretes progesterone into the blood stream. I would have my PMS clients imagine their ovaries secreting, which is similar to sweating, this hormone. All three of these clients had previously had babies. I talked to their unconscious minds, reminding them of the hormones that their bodies had produced when their babies had been living in their bodies and asked their unconscious minds to make the changes necessary to let their bodies have some of that hormonal experience now.

You may notice that the approach that I frequently use is to help the clients depend upon the wisdom and knowledge that the body has within itself. Clearly, I am assuming that the unconscious or the body itself knows what has gone on in our bodies in the past and can create that healthy experience for us.

HEALING IMAGES

The idea that our bodies know what is needed is one I use in healing requests in general. If you have an illness, you can remind your body of times you have been sick before and have recovered. Ask your unconscious to bring about that kind of healing as rapidly as it can.

For my clients, and for me personally, the most powerful image for healing is to imagine a healer. For many, that would be a religious being—Jesus, Buddha, Moses, a goddess—or a doctor, a medicine man or woman, or a deceased loved one. I begin by imagining a relaxing or a sacred place. Then I imagine the healing proceeding this way:

Imagine the healer placing his or her hands upon your head and having healing power flow into your scalp. As that power flows into your scalp, ask your unconscious to make changes in terms of biochemistry, blood flow, muscle tension, or any cleansing that needs to take place. (You might imagine the healing power as a light or as healing liquid filling each area of your body.) Let that flow down over your forehead and your eyes, making any changes in biochemistry, blood flow, or muscle tension that are needed. Let that healing power flow over your sinuses, cleansing any tissues that need to be cleansed and shrinking any tissues that need to be modified. Let that power pour into your jaw and into your ears, making any alterations that might need to be made for your health. Then let that healing power flow into your brain.

We know that the brain's biochemistry has much to do with how we feel, so as that healing power flows into your brain, you can let any changes in biochemistry or blood flow that need to occur, occur now. If any part of your brain needs to send different messages to any part of your body to promote your health, allow that to occur now.

Let the healing power flow down your windpipe, loosening the round muscles surrounding it. Feel the healing power flow down into your lungs. Allow any cleansing that needs to take place there occur now as that healing power fills every cell in your lungs.

Let that healing power flow over to your heart, filling the muscle and valves of your heart. Allow your heart to beat in a way that supports your health throughout your body, letting the blood vessels have just the appropriate amount of tension to support your health. Then let that healing power flow down your aorta, into your spleen, your liver, your gallbladder, and your kidneys. Allow that healing power to make any alterations in the blood flow, smooth muscle function, or biochemistry of any or all of those organs in such a way that supports your health.

Let that healing power flow through your stomach and your intestines, making any alterations needed for your health and comfort. Let that healing power flow into your *reproductive system, making any changes to support your health and comfort.*

Start with your neck and your shoulders and let them be filled with healing power; loosening those muscles and changing the blood flow in any way that will support your health and comfort. Then feel that healing power flow down your vertebrae, one vertebra at a time, making bands of healing surround your body. When that healing power reaches your tailbone, feel that healing power spread to your hips, filling them.

Let that healing power flow down your legs to your knees, and then to your ankles, making any changes that need to be made for your health and comfort. Then allow that healing power to flow all the way out to the tips of your toes.

Now breathe deeply as you enjoy the feeling of comfort and healing throughout your body.

If some part of your body needs particular attention, spend extra time on that area. For example, if you have back pain, imagine the healing power filling those muscles in that area and loosening the muscles so that they have just the appropriate amount of tension for health and comfort.

When you are on medications, you might suggest that your body can be particularly receptive to the helpful power of that medication, allowing the tissue that especially needs to be altered to be responsive to the medicine. When you have covered each part of your body, have the healing power concentrate in your solar plexus so that it is available for you whenever you need it.

Besides the image of touching, I use a healing light flowing from above or the Biblical image of breathing in the breath of God and having that flow throughout the body. If you are trying to get over an infection, visualize standing under a waterfall and having the water flow through and cleanse each cell.

I try to get an understanding from my doctor of what is occurring in the illness. Does fluid need to flow from or to an area? Do cells need to produce hormones or stop producing? If I can get some specifics, then I can know exactly what healing imagery I need.

Many therapists use this general healing imagery technique. I have found it to be very helpful. You may want to use it on a regular basis as part of your relaxation exercise, even if you do not have any physical problems, because it is soothing and relaxing.

INVADERS FROM OUR SPACE

Typically, two kinds of invaders affect our bodies. These are infections—bacteria and viruses—and pollens. Three techniques seem to be most effective in managing these invaders.

First, when you are in trance, imagine yourself standing in some familiar room, perhaps a place where you normally dress. Picture a circle around yourself in the floor. Upon that circle, imagine a clear acrylic shield that comes up over your head with a filtered air hole at the top. You might call this your health bubble. Ask your unconscious to let this shield protect you from viruses and pollens that surround you in your environment. Repeat this imagery from time to time.

Second, Dr. Spiegel suggests that you repeat the following phrases to yourself: *"For my body—not for me—but for my body, viruses are poison. I need my body to live. I will protect my body the same way I would protect _____."* (Insert the name of a child or someone towards whom you feel protective.)

Third, in order for your body to have difficulty with viruses or pollens, it must first respond to these invaders. Ask your unconscious to simply not respond to these. An allergic reaction is a response. You may have been exposed to the stimuli but did not respond. Ask your unconscious to help your body be indifferent to these stimuli again.

By presenting these many techniques, my goal is to stimulate your imagination in order that you may be creative with your own images. I hope you will see these as a starting point and not as a final destination. You may have many creative ideas about what would be useful to your body to promote your health. It is as if you have learned the computer's basic language and, now that you can effectively communicate with it, you can begin to experiment. Discover what programming makes the most positive changes in your health and your physical comfort.

SUMMARY: Your body has natural abilities for changing your reaction to discomfort and to illness. In pain control, several perceptual changes can lessen your experience of pain. These are time distortion, dissociation, distraction, anesthesia, and imagery in general. In illnesses, often specific changes, such as blood flow and biochemical changes, can influence healing. The unconscious can often increase these natural body responses and, therefore, speed and enhance healing.

EXERCISE: If any part of your body typically responds to tension with some kind of discomfort, imagine the following:
• a healer coming to you and placing his or her hands on your head and having that healing power spread to all parts of your body, focusing upon the part that reacts most to tension.
• exactly what physical changes need to take place for that area to be permanently more comfortable. If you have pain, practice dissociation, distraction, time distortion, anesthesia, and the control center imagery as outlined earlier in this chapter.

CHAPTER 9

ACCESSING THE DATA BASE

When you become proficient with a computer, you can hook up with giant computers that allow you to reach these database sources, as they are called. Being able to reach database sources is almost like tapping into a mystical universe. In my own experiments with my unconscious, I have used self-hypnosis and meditation to tap into a spiritual resource for myself. This experience takes two forms for me. The first is meditation. The second is getting in touch with my inner spiritual resources.

MEDITATION

Herbert Benson of the Harvard Medical School wrote an excellent book on meditation called *The Relaxation Response*. Benson's interest in meditation began with studies that he was conducting on blood pressure. He found that meditation was a powerful technique for lowering blood pressure.

Almost all the eastern religions use meditation, which is the repetition of a word or phrase as a prayer. A western religion, Catholicism, uses a repetitive prayer—the rosary. The experience of meditation can give you a peaceful, centered feeling, a stillness that is often missing from modern stress-filled life.

Meditation is different from self-hypnosis. First, the brain waves are different in that the brain waves of meditation are alpha waves and not the typical pattern of concentration found with self-hypnosis. Second, the goal of meditation is to empty your mind and not think, while the goal of self-hypnosis and imagery is to think specific helpful thoughts. Meditation is an excellent form of relaxation and a good discipline for the mind. I find the feeling in my body to be somewhat similar, and, therefore, I use meditation when I do not want to bother being creative with imagery and just want to feel more centered.

Meditation is very simple. Sit quietly, with your eyes closed and your body in a comfortable position. (I prefer to have my hands resting on my thighs.) Slow your breathing comfortably. Repeat some word or phrase as you exhale and keep repeating that word.

I recommend that you repeat the word "one." Sometimes I use the word "Yahweh," which the Bible calls the ancient name of God. The repeated word is called a *mantra*. Traditionally, mantras have nasal and long vowel sounds, but you can repeat any word that seems appropriate to you.

If thoughts come into your mind, you casually dismiss them, telling yourself that you will deal with those thoughts later. They will come into your mind less and less as you increase your mind-emptying skills. I find picturing the mantra in front of me to be helpful in avoiding thoughts. Like hypnosis, the best strategy is not to strain by berating yourself for having those interrupting thoughts, but just gently put them off until later.

Plan a meditation time in a quiet place and choose the number of minutes that you will put aside for this. I would recommend ten or twenty minutes per day. What I think is ideal is to meditate in the early evening when you first come home from work and do ten minutes of self-hypnosis in the morning as you begin your day. If twenty minutes per day will give you a longer, healthier, and happier life, what an enjoyable and useful way to have spent just those few minutes.

In years of working with people with self-esteem issues, I have found that the way to feel better about yourself is to do something that is challenging. Changing your habits to include spending twenty minutes a day of relaxation or meditation will make you feel proud of yourself in two ways. First, you will know that you have some self-control and self-discipline for simply choosing to take the time for self-improvement.

Second, the experience of taking time to relax may help you feel less stressful.

PSYCHOLOGICAL HEALING AND SELF-HYPNOSIS

One of the techniques I have used with myself and with my clients to heal from sad or upsetting events in my life is to have a ritual, like a funeral, for an event. Our society seems to be a little short on rituals, so I often make up some for myself and for clients. I have often combined the conscious planning of a ritual with the unconscious techniques of self-hypnosis and meditation to help myself and my clients complete some part of their lives. You can do this by creating a ceremony, such as a funeral, for some event and then follow it with a time of spiritual healing through imagery or meditation. For example, if a relationship ends unexpectedly, you could bury a picture of yourself with that person and then have a time of imagining a healer saying something to you about the future or the past.

When I got a divorce, I found that going to court to signify the end of a sixteen-year marriage was a brief and dissatisfying event. I decided that when the divorce was final, six months later, I would have a funeral for the marriage. I made a copy of my marriage license and then divided it into sixteen segments and arranged those segments in different groups to signify different eras of that marriage. I sat by myself in front of a fireplace with lit candles and considered each year separately. As I finished reviewing the year, I would burn the segment for that year. After all the segments were burned, I had a time of prayer and felt that the funeral for that marriage was complete. Although this did not end the sadness that accompanied the death of the marriage, it did give me a feeling that I was now in a new era and that there had been an event to begin it.

I had a 45-year-old woman client who was a devout Catholic. Against her will, she had gotten a divorce after twenty years of marriage and several children. She was very bitter and angry towards her former mate and generally towards all men. Her husband had taken nude pictures of their daughter, without the girl's knowledge, and he also had an affair with a much younger woman. These things were beyond the range of my client's forgiveness. Even before this crisis in her marriage, she had experienced difficulty enjoying sex and trusting men. The recent turn of events made the situation much worse. I put her into trance and had her imagine a relaxing place and Jesus coming to talk to her there. I suggested she ask Him for guidance and then signal me when the conversation was over. She did this and then came out of trance.

She told me that during her conversation with Christ, whom she had turned to many times previously for comfort, He had said,

"Remember, I am a man, too." This way of looking at men was a profound change for her in terms of her attitude towards men. She attended a class that I conducted a couple of years later and verified that that experience had continued to be a turning point for her. She said, "I hope you will tell other women about what Jesus said to me. It really helped me leave the past behind."

People with less conventional religious orientations can simply create their own inner guides. It is as if you personify that part of you that has wisdom. We all have times we can look back upon when we were surprised at our wisdom and courage. That could be a time when your inner guide was doing the directing. The guide could be a visual image you create yourself or the personification of strength derived from a life experience. For example, one of my clients is interested in Native American traditions and attends shamanic workshops and Native American sweat lodges. When she puts herself in trance, she finds a wise, older Native American woman who is there as her guide, answering questions and making suggestions.

To find your inner guide, go to your relaxing place. Allow yourself to get comfortable there and then say to yourself that out of the corner of your eye you begin to notice a figure coming towards you. Sometimes I choose a garden as my relaxing place. I will picture the details of the garden, including sights, sounds, smells, and feelings; then I will simply be open to whatever guide might appear. I tell myself that, at first, it will not be clear who the guide is, just as a camera can be out of focus and then adjusted in order that the image becomes clear. You might have only the sense that a guide was there or experience the guide as a voice and not a visual image. That is fine. My goal here is to encourage you to be open to whatever way that positive creative part can be available to guide you.

All of us encounter times in our lives when we feel that we are powerless to bring about the changes we want, no matter how skilled and creative we may be. Sometimes invoking the image of giving the problem away can be a relief. You might imagine the problem as a snarled mess of dirty string that you give to a higher power or your inner guide. One of the techniques I have used is to send the problem either into the ocean or into the sky. For example, you may have ended a relationship with someone, yet they continue to intrude on your mind. You might imagine putting that person on a boat and sending them out to sea or you might have Jesus or your guide launch the boat. Watch as the boat drifts farther and farther out of sight until you are not sure if that is a speck of a wave on the horizon or the boat. You might then have the guide say something to you to add to the sense of completion.

Tying a problem to a big red helium-filled balloon and letting it float up into the sky and out of sight can be another way of letting go of past problems. This technique is particularly useful for those problems about which you can do nothing at present. If something that happened long ago seems to be hanging around, you might imagine some symbol of that unpleasant time floating off into space never to be seen again.

While we have been talking about traumatic events, often you may only need to feel more centered. Sometimes, during a morning self-hypnosis, I will imagine my relaxing place and my guide coming to me with the thought for the day. With four children, a husband, a business, and a daily radio show all needing my attention, this imagery can give me a focused feeling as I start the day by concentrating on something positive.

The techniques of meditation, prayer, and imagery are all ways to clear our minds of useless thoughts and get to our inner abilities. In Zen, "monkey talk" is used as a metaphor for that little voice that blabbers on and on in the back of our minds. My husband used to call his voice the "Howard Cosell voice," constantly commenting in an annoying way about all my husband did. All the above techniques can help us rise above our monkey talk and give us a feeling of being connected to the universe.

For me, that feeling of being connected to the universe comes most often in nature. Standing watching a sunset on the ocean while thinking about the people on the other side of the sea and the vastness of the water gives me that universal feeling. Looking at a star-filled sky and thinking of all the other people on earth that are under that same heaven gives me that universal feeling. When I am in trance and I recall that feeling and those experiences, I can often recapture that centered experience and regain a sense of proportion about my normal problems of daily life. I have found that meditation, prayer, and imagery all help me gain the experience of centeredness.

SUMMARY: Two techniques using the unconscious can be particularly useful in allowing us to feel more centered and healed. The first is meditation, which involves emptying the mind of thoughts by repeating a mantra. The second is imagining an inner healer to help us resolve problems and feel in touch with a higher power.

EXERCISE: Experiment with the following:
• Meditation: Sit quietly, close your eyes, slow your breathing, and repeat "one" to yourself for ten minutes, casually dismissing thoughts as they enter your mind.
• Put yourself into a trance and ask your unconscious to imagine a wise, healing person coming to you with a thought for the day.
• Pick an unpleasant memory from your past which you need to heal. Find or make a symbol of that event or time in your past. Carry that symbol around with you for a week. Bury, burn, or toss into a river that symbol as a funeral for that time. Put yourself in trance and let your healer come to you with a word of comfort, telling you that that time never needs to have power over you again.

CHAPTER 10

THE UNCONSCIOUS MIND ON THE JOB AND IN SCHOOL

Now that you have learned all the principles about using your unconscious to help you, let's apply it to some of the most important experiences in life.

THE JOB SEARCH

In helping people find a job, one of the secrets to success is to **look** for a job. Over the years, some of my clients seemed to find jobs twice as fast as others. Their simple secret was that every day they went every place possible to find a job. A wise, older man used to say that if you put in nine hours of job hunting a day, you will have some job, if only temporary, in a week. I understand that there are times and places when not so many jobs may be available, but searching is crucial. Sometimes re-training may be necessary. For example, one client's job in the U.S. Air Force required him to select targets for attack in foreign countries. The person wisely got a master's degree in another area before retirement from the Air Force.

If going for the interview is the scary part for you, use your unconscious to help. If possible, prior to going to the interview, go to the place that you are supposed to have the interview. Look at the setting as discreetly as you can, in order that you can use specific imagery about that location to help you. Perhaps you can see only a waiting room. Notice physical details, such as a picture on the wall or a chair. When you put yourself in a trance in preparation for the interview, you can tell yourself that the sight of that picture or that chair will be your signal to breathe deeply and to go into a trance for the job interview. If you know the specific person who is to do the interviewing, you could tell yourself that the sight of that person will be your signal to go into trance.

Prepare yourself for the interview by writing down what questions you may be asked. Then go into trance and imagine answering them successfully. You can always peek at the questions if you need to; therefore, keep them in sight when you put yourself in trance. You may answer the questions differently in the interview, but the important concept is to imagine success. While you are in a trance, imagine being told that you are hired. Ask your unconscious to help you perform the appropriate actions to bring that about.

Remember, your unconscious cannot do all the work. You have to fill out the application, show up appropriately dressed, and be on time. Then your unconscious can help you in the interview.

CONCENTRATION AND ORGANIZATION

When you have a project to get done at work or school, one of the first things to do is to write on a piece of paper all the elements of the project. At this point, worrying about the order would not be helpful. Before you go to sleep, ask your unconscious to organize the project for you while you sleep. When you awaken, write down the outline that comes to mind. If some part of the project requires writing, such as submitting a proposal, again ask your unconscious to organize this during your sleep. Good ideas are much like pregnancy. It takes a while for them to germinate. Thank goodness most ideas don't take nine months!

I have always found that the most powerful tool for being organized is to prioritize. Lately, I have seen more and more articles about how increasingly busy our lives seem to be—the frantic family syndrome. The labor-saving devices that were supposed to give us leisure time have provided us time for more and more labors. Since I am a working wife and mother, for me, and probably for you, some tasks will be left uncompleted. To try to help the situation, I sit down for about twenty minutes every two or three days and make a list of the things I need to accomplish. Usually, I rank these in order of importance, but if I am feeling overwhelmed, then I will look these over before I go to sleep and organize them as soon as I wake up.

One of the best pieces of advice I ever received from the many time management books I have read is the idea that completing tasks brings energy. If I come home to many undone tasks, such as unfolded laundry, unwashed dishes, or unpaid bills, I can feel the energy drain from me as I look at those tasks. If I complete even one small task, the energy returns and more is available for the other tasks. Start with the most important task and take it all the way to completion. That will give you the most energy.

Most of the adults I know have had to go back to school to advance in their careers. The two major tasks of school, after you have committed to putting in the time necessary to input the information into your brain, are concentration and managing anxiety on tests.

If your job or studies require concentration, and you have a noisy or distracting environment, put yourself in trance and pick some object on your desk or in your work space that will serve as your signal to begin ignoring outside noises and concentrating. When I have a writing job to do, I tell myself that the signal to begin concentrating will be the sight of the screen on the computer monitor. As soon as the monitor comes on, I find that distractions seem to disappear.

In putting myself into trance before studying, I also suggest to myself that I will be pleasantly surprised at how easily the material organizes in my mind into a mental outline. I usually go back over any textbook material to see how the author planned the structure of the information, so that may help me keep it organized in my mind too.

The two areas that you can focus on to be better students are concentration during studying and test taking. For studying, ask your unconscious to pick some signal that will remind your unconscious to begin concentrating. Before you sit down to study, put yourself in trance in whatever resting position you choose. Tell your unconscious that the signal to begin concentrating will be the sight of the particular book you need to study, the feeling of the pen, the sight of the computer keyboard, or whatever is an appropriate signal for your situation. Say that outside noises will only help you to concentrate more (an important suggestion in a dormitory). Tell yourself that you will be pleasantly surprised at how well the material organizes itself in your mind and how easily you remember what you have studied. Specify, in trance, how long a time period (for example, an hour) you will continue to concentrate on studying. Say to yourself that you will feel comfortably energized and refreshed when you have finished studying.

One man I did hypnosis with was working on his doctorate and dealing with all the stresses of normal adult life as well (job, relationships, children, unpaid bills). As part of his concentration, I had him imagine going into a compartment where he was only to do one thing—study. This worked so well for him in his imagination that he even arranged a small study room. There he could physically compartmentalize his work, no longer trying to study on a desk that had unanswered personal correspondence and bills to be paid sitting beside the text to be studied.

Limit the amount of time you plan to study. Take a break every so often. It will keep you from feeling drained and keep the energy level up for more studying.

With very long projects that require months or more to prepare, two things help maintain energy. The first is the practical matter of simply dividing the task into smaller, do-able tasks. For example, if you have a long report, a thesis, or proposal to write, outline it and set small goals for yourself, such as completion of the introduction by a certain date, etc. The second thing I have found useful is to imagine that the project is done. Imagine the reactions you will have and think of how good you will feel having completed the task. If you don't have an appreciative audience, focus on your own pride. I know an attorney who realized that no one was going to notice just how brilliant the contracts he designed were, so he made a point of looking at a completed contract and saying, "Good job!"

If you reach a block in a big project, you can apply your knowledge of dream programming. Use as your incubation sentence, "Let me know what I need to do to finish this project." Remember to ask yourself before the dream incubation sentence what the advantages would be of finishing or not finishing the project. It may be that the thing you would have to do after this project is complete is the barrier to completion.

TEST ANXIETY

For tests, I would use the imagery of having just the appropriate amount of tension. Being utterly relaxed in a test-taking situation decreases memory and motivation. Too much tension will interfere with memory. The best phrase, therefore, is "an appropriate amount." Choose a signal to begin, such as the feeling of the number two pencil in your hand. Take three deep breaths before starting and tell yourself that you will be pleasantly surprised both at how easily the material organizes in your mind and at your recall of the material. Finally, imagine yourself enjoying the satisfaction of feeling good about your performance when you complete the test.

Imagine success on a test. Think about how you will feel when you have finished the test to your own satisfaction. If it would help you, imagine how others might feel about your achievement. Remember, it is hard to do anything if you cannot do it first in your imagination.

GETTING ALONG WITH OTHERS

Having a job outside your home or going to school with other human beings will result in conflict at some time. It may be slightly easier to handle the conflict if you are the boss, but even then it is still a challenge.

How do you use the unconscious to handle conflict with a boss or teacher? One of the first ways is to use relaxation to keep yourself calm with that person. Before you go to work or class, put yourself in a trance and go to your relaxing place. Then instruct your unconscious that the signal for you to have those relaxing feelings will be the sight, thought, or sound of the person you think might upset you.

Often we catastrophise to ourselves about how terrible things would be if we lost a particular job or left school. This automatically defeats attempts at relaxation. In reality, job changes sometimes force us to seek new, more appropriate goals, such as going back to school, or applying for a more responsible position. Dropping out of school until I had a clearer image of what I wanted to do saved me from interior design, which might have been fun, but not as much fun as this is for me. Put yourself into a trance and let your unconscious help you imagine what good things could come out of such a change. Trusting that there are always options helps you avoid feeling trapped and helps you feel more relaxed about a problem you might have with a specific person.

One of the techniques I use when I find myself in conflict with a coworker is to notice our pattern of interaction. I ask myself, "What do I usually do in response to what they usually do?" For example, if I have a super-sensitive employee, do I usually avoid telling them what I want? When I notice that I am not saying what I think, I plan a relaxed forum for communication, such as eating lunch together. My unconscious can help by rehearsing the scene and by reminding me to stay relaxed whenever I see, think of, or hear that person.

Dream programming can also be useful in a conflict situation. You might create a dream incubation phrase like: "What is it about this person that sets me off?" or "What do I need to do to be more comfortable around this person?"

Never be afraid to use your imagination to set your goals. Looking back over my life, I realize how surprised I am that a woman who thought she would be content raising kids and being a homemaker ended up getting a doctorate, running a counseling center, having a radio show, writing books, and doing trainings. Twenty years ago, I really did not have the slightest idea of what was in store for me. My experience makes me realize how many possibilities exist for us if we are willing to use our unconscious minds, take risks, and change actions.

SUMMARY: While actions are the key to success on the job and in school, your unconscious mind can help you by improving your concentration and helping you relax in stressful situations, such as on tests or with an individual who irritates you.

Dreams and creativity during the sleeping state can help you with projects and term papers. You can ask for that help by formal dream programming or simply asking your unconscious to work on something while you sleep.

EXERCISE: Make a list of your goals for this week. Put them beside your bed and ask your unconscious to organize them into priorities for the next few days.

Write down what object you will use for concentration in each setting you are trying to improve. Do self-hypnosis and remind yourself of this signal.

Imagine success at whatever you are trying to accomplish—school or work—and ask your unconscious in trance to help you accomplish that goal.

CHAPTER 11

LOVE AND THE UNCONSCIOUS

FALLING IN LOVE

Keeping in mind the idea that it is very difficult to do things that you cannot imagine, what would you need to do to find a person to love? Start with imagining him or her coming into your life. Many of the people who do not find relationships are blocked because they cannot visualize someone responding to them and do not even notice when it is happening. Begin by imagining many different situations in which you might initiate a relationship.

Some people are good at meeting people. My daughter Angie had a friend in high school who was very good at initiating relationships. My daughter's friend was a flirt. Angie was shy and talked to me about what she needed to do to get relationships started. I said, "Imagine you are your friend Judy. Think about the way she talks, what she says, the way she looks at a guy, the way she smiles. Those are behaviors that you can learn, too, not magical inborn powers. Notice how she acts and then rehearse doing the same actions in your mind." This pointed my daughter in the right direction, and she improved at being able to meet people to date.

Ask your unconscious for help. Earlier, we talked about finding out what purpose a behavior served. If you find yourself isolated from relationships, perhaps this is a way of keeping yourself safe. A favorite phrase of a friend of mine is "No guts, no glory!" Getting your unconscious to help you get out where you can meet people and start talking may let you in for some of the glory. When people asked the comedian, Elayne Boosler, how on earth she met a new boyfriend so quickly after breaking up with the old one, she replied that her secret was that she left her apartment.

Your unconscious might work while you are asleep to explore what you need to do differently. You could ask your unconscious to give you some ideas about what you need to do to start a relationship or you might ask your unconscious to give you some creative ideas to get over some roadblock in a relationship. Creativity from your unconscious mind is one of the ways to get over a difficulty in a relationship.

GETTING OVER THE HURDLES

I am known in my community for marital therapy. I use many practical communication techniques to treat relationship problems. The skills I teach my clients solve nearly all the relationship problems that people bring into my office. However, when I do reach an impasse, I use unconscious techniques to find out what the difficulty is and what creative approach might work. For example, when a client wants to enjoy sex, but doing the standard sex therapy treatment does not bring about change, then hypnosis might be in order.

Sometimes, things happen in relationships that you need to forget and leave behind. For example, if someone has had an affair, the unconscious can help. One woman I was working with imagined sending her husband's secretary, with whom he had had an affair, off into outer space to get over her feelings of distress. All the practical tasks had been done: the secretary had been fired, the husband was recommitted to the relationship, he had done everything he could to help the relationship and had apologized, but the memory was haunting her. Putting the wife in trance and sending the secretary into a black hole in outer space somehow gave the wife the distance she needed to get on with the relationship.

One day my husband and I had quibbled over the usual dual-career issue: who is doing what around the house. At the end of the day he said,

"We just seem to be stuck. Let's just put this day in a basket, attach the basket to a red, helium-filled balloon, and send if off." I was quite agreeable to this, and as we went to sleep, that futile argument floated away.

DREAMING YOUR TROUBLES AWAY

Dreams may have a message for you about your relationship. Earlier, I mentioned that I had a vivid dream about a revolution that was about to happen just before I went into the crisis that led to my divorce. While I don't see every dream I have as a warning, I don't ignore warning dreams either.

I have a pattern in relationships that when things get intensely intimate, I get scared that something will go wrong. Recently, I was feeling more in love with my husband than I usually feel. I started having repetitive dreams about my husband having an affair or being attracted to someone else. This did not fit with reality, since he seems crazy about me and was saying that he was happier than he had ever been in his life. I asked my unconscious to have a dream that would tell me why I was having the affair dreams. I then had a dream about being on a beautiful nature trip in the mountains and having an accident that was a close call; that is, while there were no injuries, someone could have been hurt. While I considered this to have several possible interpretations, the one that fit best for me was that I am skeptical about human nature. Seeing couple after couple wherein one of them is having or has had an affair leads to discouraged feelings about human nature. As my unconscious was saying, human nature can be a scary thing.

I have also asked my unconscious to have a dream about something creative I could do with a block in relationships. If you are having a repetitive problem in a relationship, ask your unconscious to let you have a dream that will give you a new approach to the difficulty. You may be surprised at what new ideas you come up with through your unconscious.

WHEN YOU NEED TO NOT RESPOND

Often I will have a client who is dealing with a spouse who verbally attacks without warning. I use the technique I mentioned earlier of the client's practicing the imagery of being surrounded by a clear acrylic shield during hypnosis. Imagine that spouse shooting arrows labeled with the names you have been called. Picture those arrows falling to the ground blunted and broken.

Usually I will get to work with both partners in a relationship, and we can change the pattern so that the verbal arrows are not shot in the first place. If you have not been able to get a change in response from your spouse and you still wish to maintain the marriage, changing your response may help.

A relationship can be the best or the worst thing that ever happened to you. By using your creative abilities available from your unconscious, you can mobilize your resources to obtain, foster, and keep a relationship.

If you wish further information read *Rewriting Love Stories: Brief Marital Therapy,* the book I wrote with my husband, Bill O'Hanlon, on relationships (1992, W.W. Norton publisher) or listen to the audio tape, *Love Is a Verb,* of our relationship class for the public, which can be purchased through the Hudson Center in Omaha. (See back pages for details.)

SUMMARY: This chapter applied the techniques of the previous chapters to your love life. In initiating relationships, imagery and relaxation are ways of coping with fears. Techniques for getting over difficulties in love are provided through dreams and asking the unconscious for help as well as through self-hypnosis.

EXERCISE: Put yourself in trance and imagine how you would like for your relationship to be. Ask your unconscious to make whatever alterations are necessary to have that relationship. Ask your unconscious to allow you to deal creatively with your partner.

CHAPTER 12

ENJOYING YOUR USER-FRIENDLY UNCONSCIOUS

I hope that you have already experimented with the techniques in this book or will go back now and begin working your way through the exercises.

As a therapist, I have favored two approaches over the many years of helping people: getting people to do something different, which is often the quickest road to change; and using indirect suggestions and the power of the unconscious to help people change. I have spent much time considering what constitutes a "healthy" person, and balance is the key. I have emphasized the uses of the unconscious as a primary tool in bringing about changes, but I have also mentioned the necessity of simply taking action. My hope is that you will find a balance between self-understanding, friendship with your unconscious, and the necessity for actions.

Many personality theorists, particularly Jungian analysts, make a division between extroverts and introverts. Extroverts get their energy from actions and doing. Introverts need time alone for self-examination. Maturity may have something to do with developing both sides of the personality. My hope for you is that, if you need to, you will take actions to change or enrich your external life and, at the same time, you would also systematically develop and care for your inner life.

To nurture these two aspects of the self, you may need to manage your schedule so that you have time alone to develop your relationship with the unconscious. Just as it is easier to develop an exercise program if you exercise at the same time each week, you can develop your unconscious by practicing self-hypnosis and dream interpretation on a regular schedule.

I have been using unconscious techniques since I was a teenager. It is hard for me to imagine how my life might have been if I had not used these skills. Having a user-friendly unconscious has consistently added to my life. It has been most valuable to me as I went through transitions: becoming an adult, getting through school, becoming a mother, going through a divorce, and entering a new marriage.

When I decided to write this book, one of the things that motivated me was to have a guidebook that would share the things that I had learned with my friends and my children. My oldest child Angie read an early draft of this book while she was in college. In the process of editing it for me and making suggestions, she mastered self-hypnosis. A year later, while warming up for a women's rugby game, two men in a men's division finals rugby match collided and bounced out of bounds and into my daughter, causing a compound fracture of both the bones in her lower leg. She said that she was immediately able to put herself in trance while waiting for the ambulance because she had read this book and practiced self-hypnosis. In many ways, that alone has made my efforts worthwhile. While I hope you never have such a dramatic use for this information, my wish for you is that you enjoy the pleasure and power that comes from having a user-friendly unconscious.

This book has emphasized do-it-yourself hypnosis, problem-solving, dream analysis, and general self-exploration, but at times you may need outside help. When should you seek outside help? When a problem interferes severely with a major part of your life: your health, your job, your relationship with a spouse, or your relationships with your children. By interfering severely, I mean when your problems are so severe that you might be heading toward losing some aspect of your life that you value, or when you experience unhappiness for longer than a couple of months. I myself have sought therapy at three different times in my life: when I was in college, when I realized that my first marriage was in trouble, and when I separated from my first husband. Having a good therapist helped me arrive at creative solutions more quickly and put the difficulties of my life in perspective.

Therapy can help you to know what is "normal." It is normal to hurt badly when a marriage breaks up. As a former friend of mine said, "If you have the choice of getting a stick in the eye or getting a divorce, take the stick. You'll get over it quicker." It is normal to grieve when someone dies. Seeing an experienced therapist helps normalize loss and grief difficulties.

Selecting a therapist is sometimes a challenge. Academic credentials are of considerable significance to your insurance company, but in directing The Hudson Center for Brief Therapy since 1975, I have not noticed a correlation between academic training and excellence of therapeutic interventions. I would, however, not seek a therapist who did not have at least a master's degree in counseling or social work. I have a doctorate, but I had been a therapist for several years before I received my doctorate, and I do not think it significantly improved my therapeutic skills. I might suggest that you look for someone who has had special training as a marriage and family therapist. Membership in the American Association for Marriage and Family Therapy is a good indicator that the therapist has extra training. I would not likely see someone for a marital problem who did not have that training. Since many other difficulties tend to link up with family problems, that might be a credential to look for whenever you are seeking a therapist. These are my biases.

You might also get a recommendation from someone who has actually seen that therapist. A customer is someone who knows firsthand whether this therapist was helpful or not. If for some reason you just do not like that therapist by the end of the second session, see someone else. You need to be comfortable.

Many therapists with credentials do not know hypnosis. I consider hypnosis to be an essential skill that a therapist should have available. Since very few states license hypnotherapists, you will simply have to ask your potential therapists what training they have had in hypnosis and how often they use it.

I would steer clear of anyone who calls themselves a hypnotherapist but who does not have an advanced degree in some area of mental health. I had a client once who went to a local "hypnotherapist" who did not have a legitimate degree. The client's goal was to lose weight. The "hypnotherapist" told her in trance that her body would self-destruct if she did not follow his instructions. Without some organization, such as the American Association for Marriage and Family Therapy, the American Psychological Association, or the National Association of Social Workers, policing the therapist's work, you have no assurance that you will receive ethical treatment. Of course membership is only a little assurance, but at least that is another piece of information you might consider in selecting a therapist.

I think it is a good idea to get a routine physical from a physician first, particularly if the difficulty could be described as a mood problem. However, my experience has been that the more medications you avoid, the better. Remember that medications don't act just at the site of the difficulty unless injected right in it. Sometimes a physician can recommend a therapist, but unless you are hearing voices or are too dysfunctional to even read this, I would avoid a psychiatrist unless it is for proper medication. Psychologists have a bachelor's degree as well as a master's degree in counseling or psychology and a doctorate in psychology. They are prepared to treat people with everyday difficulties, as are clinical social workers and master's level counselors. Psychiatrists have a medical degree and advanced training in treating people who are typically in mental hospitals. These are severely disturbed people who think bizarre thoughts, such as God is directly talking to them, or who think the neighbors are trying to kill them, etc. People with master's degrees in counseling and social work are usually trained to do therapy. The doctorate-level therapist has some advanced training in therapy but usually the extra training involves testing, which may not be needed in most typical adult problems. While there are exceptions to all these suggestions, I wanted you to have somewhere to start if you are interested in finding a therapist who could help you.

I have a strong bias towards solution-oriented therapy, also called possibility therapy. This is usually short-term therapy and would not necessarily deal with any childhood problems. The average stay in therapy at my counseling center is 5.4 sessions, so I would be very hesitant to go to someone who tells you that the therapy will take a year. Look for a therapist who will help you change your patterns as quickly as possible and to whom you like to talk. Remember, you are the best expert on your problem and you are hiring the therapist to help. If you are not getting helped or are getting worse, save your insurance company's and your money. (If you would like to know more about what solution-oriented therapy is like, you could read *In Search of Solutions* by O'Hanlon and Weiner-Davis.)

Throughout this book, I have compared becoming friends with your computer to becoming friends with your unconscious mind. I have come to depend so much on my computer that I probably need a computer-dependency program to deal with my addiction to this helpful tool. I hope that same degree of comfort with your unconscious is now or soon will be available for you. Your unconscious has power and convenience similar to a computer. I strongly urge you to play with your unconscious. That is how I learned how to use the computer, and how you can learn to be friends with your unconscious.

One of the strong messages I want you to get from this book is that you can trust yourself. You can trust yourself on a conscious level, and you can trust yourself on an unconscious level.

A second message is to experiment. Experiment in doing different things in terms of the actions you take and experiment in doing different things with your unconscious. The answers are both inside you and in the actions you take or stop taking. Thank you for letting me be part of the experiment and participate in your journey.

SUMMARY: Practice. If you need help, find someone with a good reputation as a therapist who also does hypnosis and has credentials from a reputable educational institution.

Trust yourself. If you have gotten only one thing from this book, I hope that it is that you have discovered resources inside that are available to you when you want to use them. Good luck!

REFERENCES

Andreas, S. & Andreas, C. (1989). *Heart of the mind: Engaging your inner power to change with neuro-linguistic programming.* Moab, Utah: Real People Press.

Bandler, R. & Grinder, J. (1979). *Frogs into princes: Neuro linguistic programming.* Moab, Utah: Real People Press.

Benson, H. (1976). *The relaxation response.* New York: Avon.

Delaney, G. (1988). *Living your dreams.* San Francisco: Harper & Row.

Hilgard, E. (1968). *The experience of hypnosis.* New York: Harbinger.

Hudson, P. & O'Hanlon, W. (1992). *Rewriting love stories: Brief marital therapy.* New York: Norton.

Maltz, M. (1963). *Psychocybernetics.* Englewood Cliffs, New Jersey: Prentice-Hall.

O'Hanlon, W. (1987). *Taproots: Underlying principles of Milton Erickson's therapy and hypnosis.* New York: Norton.

O'Hanlon, W. & Weiner-Davis, M. (1989). *In search of solutions: A new direction in psychotherapy.* New York: Norton.

O'Hanlon, W. & Martin, M. (1992). *Solution-oriented hypnosis: An Ericksonian approach.* New York: Norton.

Perls, F. (1974). *Gestalt therapy verbatim.* New York: Bantam.

Spiegel, H. & Spiegel, D. (1978). *Trance and treatment: Clinical uses of hypnosis.* New York: Basic Books.

Wolpe, J. (1973). *The practice of behavior therapy.* Elmsford, New York: Pergamon Press.

INDEX

KEEP YOUR FEET MOVING

A LIVELY TAPE FILLED WITH ENGAGING STORIES FROM A MASTER STORYTELLER

Tape Includes:
* *FAVORITE TEACHING STORIES FROM BILL O'HANLON* *

* *ORIGINAL MUSIC BY BILL O'HANLON* *